GETTYSBURG

National Military Park

by Sue Bradford Edwards

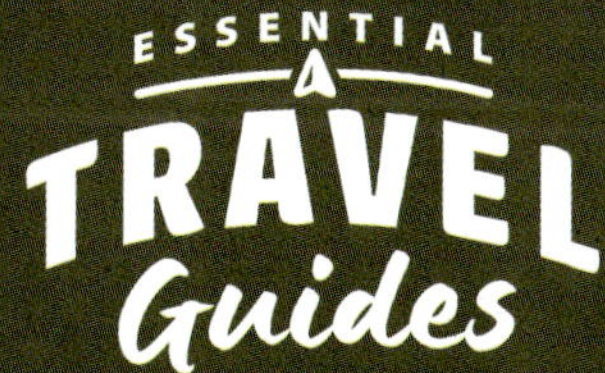

An Imprint of Abdo Publishing
abdobooks.com

ABDOBOOKS.COM

Published by Abdo Publishing, a division of ABDO, PO Box 398166, Minneapolis, Minnesota 55439.

Printed in China.
052025
092025

Cover Photo: Gary Saxe/Shutterstock Images
Interior Photos: Universal History Archive/Universal Images Group/Getty Images, 4–5; Library of Congress, 6, 68; Bildagentur-online/Universal Images Group/Getty Images, 9; Science & Society Picture Library/Getty Images, 13; Historical/Corbis Historical/Getty Images, 14; Buyenlarge/Archive Photos/Getty Images, 16; George Sheldon/Shutterstock Images, 18–19; Tim Sloan/AFP/Getty Images, 20, 62; Maurice Savage/Alamy, 23; Brian Cahn/ZUMAPRESS.com/ZUMA Press, Inc./Alamy, 24; Zack Frank/Shutterstock Images, 26, 32; James Brunker/Alamy, 28–29; Steve Allen/Allen Creative/Alamy, 31; Jon Bilous/Shutterstock Images, 35; William Silver/Shutterstock Images, 36, 61; miralex/iStock Unreleased/Getty Images, 39; Eight Arts Photography/Alamy, 40; Craig Fildes/Moment/Getty Images, 42–43; Richard Green/Commercial/Alamy, 44; catnap72/E+/Getty Images, 47; Shutterstock Images, 50, 66–67, 92, 94; Dennis MacDonald/Shutterstock Images, 54–55; Mark Summerfield/Alamy, 56–57; Buyenlarge UIG/Universal Images Group North America LLC/Alamy, 58; Heritage Art/Heritage Images/Heritage Image Partnership Ltd/Alamy, 65; Walt Bilous/Shutterstock Images, 71, 76; Matt Rourke/AP Images, 75; Matt McClain/The Washington Post/Getty Images, 78–79, 81; Andre Jenny/Alamy, 83; Amy Cicconi/Alamy, 86; Jason Martz/National Park Service, 88–89; John Michnowicz/Shutterstock Images, 97; James Kirkikis/Shutterstock Images, 98; Red Line Editorial, 101

Editor: Laura Stickney
Series Designer: Joshua Olson

Library of Congress Control Number: 2024948558

PUBLISHER'S CATALOGING-IN-PUBLICATION DATA

Names: Edwards, Sue Bradford, author.
Title: Gettysburg National Military Park / by Sue Bradford Edwards
Description: Minneapolis, Minnesota: Abdo Publishing, 2026 | Series: Essential travel guides | Includes online resources and index.
Identifiers: ISBN 9781098297091 (lib. bdg.) | ISBN 9798384919612 (ebook)
Subjects: LCSH: Gettysburg National Military Park (Pa.)--Juvenile literature. | Travel--Juvenile literature. | United States--Guidebooks--Juvenile literature. | Battlefields--Juvenile literature. | Historic sites--Juvenile literature.
Classification: DDC 917.48--dc23

CONTENTS

CHAPTER
ONE

THE BATTLE OF GETTYSBURG

When Abraham Lincoln was elected US president in 1860, he had been running for office with the promise that slavery would not extend into new territory as the United States expanded west. At this time in US history, people of African descent could be enslaved in 15 states and seven territories.[1] Territories were areas of land that were part of the United States but had not yet become states.

At the time of Lincoln's election, slavery had existed in the United States for more than two hundred years. Enslaved people had first been brought there in 1619. Since then, slavery had grown into a widespread practice, especially in Southern states. But by 1860, 18 states had enacted laws that made it illegal to enslave a person.[2]

During the American Civil War, President Abraham Lincoln, *wearing top hat*, visited several major battlefields. In October 1862, Lincoln met with Union Army officers at the site of the Battle of Antietam in Maryland.

Many people in Southern states were not happy about Lincoln's plan to stop the spread of slavery. In December 1860, South Carolina seceded from the United States. Six other Southern slave states did the same in early 1861. Four more states followed later that year.[3] Together, these states formed the Confederate States of America. This action led to the American Civil War (1861–1865), in which the Confederacy, or the South, fought the Union, or the North.

Before the Battle of Gettysburg, Major General George Gordon Meade fought in several other major battles, including the Battle of Antietam in 1862 and the Battle of Chancellorsville in 1863.

The war was fought over two things. One was whether slavery would be allowed in the United States. The other was whether the country was an indivisible nation or if states could secede from it. The bloodiest battle of the war was the Battle of Gettysburg, which took place in Pennsylvania from July 1 to July 3, 1863.

Before the Battle

The Battle of Gettysburg was preceded by the Battle of Chancellorsville, which took place from April 30 to May 6, 1863, in Virginia. In this battle, Major General Joseph Hooker led 130,000 Union soldiers against General Robert E. Lee's forces.[4] Although Lee's force was half the size of Hooker's, Lee defeated the larger force. This victory enabled Lee to move his forces into the North.

Lee believed that if he invaded a free Northern state, the Union Army would follow him there. Many battles of the war had already been fought in Virginia, which meant that Virginia farmers had been unable to plant and harvest crops. Supplies for the Confederate Army were running low, so Lee led his army to Pennsylvania to give Virginia farmers an opportunity to plant crops.

Hooker followed Lee north but didn't force him into battle, so President Lincoln replaced Hooker with Major

General George Gordon Meade on June 28. This was the same day that Lee's forces reached Pennsylvania's Susquehanna River. When Lee learned Meade was nearby, Lee moved his army toward Gettysburg, Pennsylvania.

Around 2,400 people lived in Gettysburg, and they knew what would happen as the two armies moved through the area.[5] If fighting broke out, people would be in danger. Soldiers would also search markets, businesses, and farms for supplies, including shoes, clothing, and medicine. They would take residents' food, water, and horses. While some residents left the area, many others hid in their cellars.

The Brian Farm

When Abraham Brian returned to his farm after the Battle of Gettysburg, he discovered that it had been near some of the worst fighting. His home had been damaged by both gunshots and artillery shells. His crops and orchard were destroyed. His animals were missing too. The troops had also left 106 graves behind. Brian calculated the value of what he had lost at $1,028.[6] This is equal to about $25,578 in 2024.[7] The government paid him $15.[8] This is about $373 in 2024.[9]

Among those who fled Gettysburg were many Black citizens. They were afraid of being captured by the Confederate forces. Even before the war started, Southern patrols often crossed into free states and kidnapped free Black people, claiming they were enslaved.

In 1845, one such patrol kidnapped Catherine Payne and her children, who had been formerly enslaved but

During the Battle of Gettysburg, most soldiers fought with rifle muskets, pistols, and carbines. But cannons, swords, and bayonets were also used.

legally freed. A series of legal battles secured their release. Later, Payne settled in Gettysburg and married farmer Abraham Brian. As the armies moved into Gettysburg, the Brians fled. Owen Robinson, who sold oysters and ice cream, and veterinarian Basil Biggs also left the area.

The Battle Begins

The fighting at Gettysburg began on July 1 when a division of the Confederate Army led by Major General Henry Heth marched toward the town to seize supplies. A Union cavalry force engaged them in battle. The smaller force of 20,000 Union troops was pushed back through town by 30,000 Confederate troops and took up a position at Cemetery Hill south of town.[10]

On July 2, Meade moved his generals into position to form a secure three-mile (5 km) line along the hills and ridges south of Gettysburg.[11] At 3:30 p.m., the Confederates attacked as Lee ordered a heavy assault. Fierce fighting ensued at Devil's Den, Little Round Top, the Wheatfield, the Peach Orchard, and Cemetery Ridge. Even though Confederate forces gained ground at both ends, the Union forces held strong positions as night fell.

Fighting resumed on July 3 with aggressive Confederate assaults. This occurred because Lee assumed the Union forces had been seriously weakened and could be overcome. But the Union troops were determined to regain the ground they had lost the day before and continued to fight. A Confederate infantry force of 12,500 men fought their way up Cemetery Ridge, but they were advancing across a one-mile (1.6 km)

John Burns

John Burns, a 70-year-old Gettysburg civilian, was a veteran of the War of 1812 (1812–1815). In this war, the United States and Britain fought over maritime trade. Burns tried to enlist in the Union Army when the American Civil War started, but he was sent home because officials thought he was too old to fight. When the Battle of Gettysburg started, Burns asked a wounded soldier if he could use his rifle. He used the weapon to fight alongside Union troops on July 1, 1863, protecting soldiers by acting as a sharpshooter. Burns was wounded three times during the battle but survived. When President Lincoln later visited Gettysburg, he asked to meet Burns.

open field.[12] Union cannons fired on them during the advance. By the end of the charge, the Confederates had suffered casualties of 60 percent.[13]

When the remaining Confederate soldiers retreated, Meade didn't order a counterattack, fearing the damage that Confederate cannons would do to his own troops when crossing the open fields. After Lee discovered how many men he had lost at Gettysburg, he withdrew his forces and retreated south on the afternoon of July 4. The Union had won the battle. The victory was a turning point in the war, reversing a year of victories for Lee and the Confederacy.

After the Battle

By the end of the Battle of Gettysburg, the two armies had suffered between 46,000 and 51,000 casualties in all.[14] This included dead and wounded men and captured and missing men. Only one civilian was killed during the battle. The Wade family had been supplying Union soldiers with bread and water.

"They were at once enveloped in a dense cloud of smoke and dust. . . . Arms, heads, blankets, guns and knapsacks were thrown and tossed into the clear air. . . . A moan went up from the field, distinctly to be heard amid the storm of battle.[15]

—US Lieutenant Colonel Franklin Sawyer, describing the Confederate advance on July 3

On July 3, the home where they were staying was hit with more than 150 rounds of Confederate gunfire. Jennie Wade was in the kitchen kneading a fresh batch of dough when a minié ball passed through two doors and into the kitchen, killing her.[16]

More than 170,000 men had descended on the area surrounding the town. By the time the armies left, water and food were in short supply, and 21,000 wounded people and 11,000 dead people were left behind. At least 45 private homes and every public building in Gettysburg had been turned into hospitals.[17] At St. Francis Xavier Roman Catholic Church, boards laid across pews served as temporary beds, and surgeons set up an operating table in the vestibule.

The US Sanitary Commission, an aid organization similar to today's American Red Cross, and the Christian Commission set up headquarters in town. These groups provided supplies and food. They brought doctors and nurses to tend to the wounded. But families of soldiers also arrived looking for loved ones. Curious onlookers came too. All these people had to be housed and fed.

The Union Army realized that some men were too badly hurt to be moved to existing hospitals. Because of this, the army built Camp Letterman, a hospital camp located 1.5 miles (2.4 km) east of Gettysburg. At one time, more than 1,600 wounded soldiers from both the Union and Confederate armies were housed there.[18]

Another problem was dealing with the dead. Approximately 5,000 dead horses were burned in a slow, putrid process.[19] Many of the Union casualties had been hastily buried by surviving soldiers before the armies left the area. Several days after the battle, Elizabeth

Hundreds of hospital tents were set up at Camp Letterman to accommodate wounded soldiers. Surgeons performed amputations at operating tents in the camp.

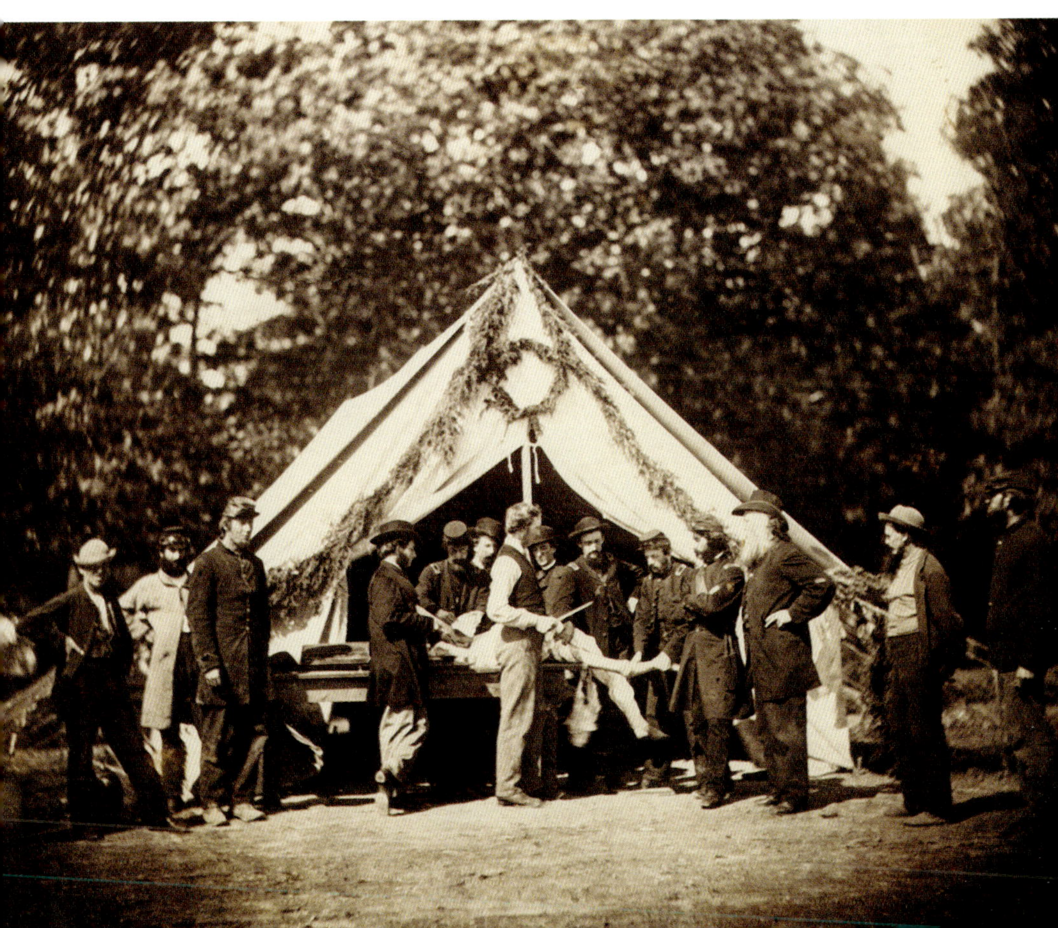

Thorn received a letter from David McConaughy. He was president of Gettysburg's Evergreen Cemetery.

Thorn's husband was the cemetery's caretaker but was serving as a Union soldier. In the letter, McConaughy wrote, "We will bury the soldiers in cemetery for awhile so you go for that piece of ground and commence sticking off lots and graves as fast as you can make them." Thorn was six months pregnant and caring for her elderly father at the time. But she and her father buried 105 soldiers.[20]

Many other graves lay scattered throughout the countryside. Heavy rains had fallen on July 4, and

Photographers documented the aftermath of the Battle of Gettysburg. One 1863 photo shows the bodies of dead Confederate soldiers lying in incomplete graves on the battlefield.

additional rainfall in the following months unearthed many shallow graves in which soldiers had been hastily buried. Gettysburg resident David Wills, an attorney, suggested to Pennsylvania governor Andrew Curtin that the state fund a cemetery for the fallen soldiers. Curtin formed a committee, which included Wills, and the committee members purchased 17 acres (6.9 ha) of land next to Evergreen Cemetery.[21]

On October 27, 1863, interments in the new cemetery began. Local Black residents who had returned to the area were tasked with disinterring earlier burials, placing each set of remains in a wooden coffin, and reburying them in the new cemetery. This cemetery was only for Union soldiers. Confederate remains were later shipped to Southern cemeteries.

Wills organized a ceremony to dedicate the cemetery. Two speakers, politician Edward Everett and President Lincoln, were scheduled to speak at the ceremony. President Lincoln had little time for public events because of his busy schedule, but he made time for the ceremony and finished writing his speech after arriving in town on November 18. The ceremony took place the following day on Cemetery Hill. Approximately 15,000 people attended the ceremony. Edward Everett spoke for about two hours.

There is only one confirmed photograph of President Abraham Lincoln visiting Gettysburg. It shows a crowd in front of a platform on the day of the cemetery dedication ceremony, and Lincoln's head is visible toward the center.

In contrast, Lincoln's Gettysburg Address was only two minutes long.[22]

Before and after the cemetery dedication, one Gettysburg resident worked to memorialize the events that had taken place in the town. On September 5, 1863, David McConaughy had worked with local citizens to create the Gettysburg Battlefield Memorial Association. In 1867 and 1868, the state legislature gave this organization $3,000 to purchase portions of the battlefield, including parts of Culp's Hill, Cemetery Hill, and the top of Little Round Top.[23]

In 1895, the Battlefield Memorial Association transferred ownership of the area to the government. A federally appointed commission of Civil War veterans directed the development of the site as a monument to both armies that fought there. In 1933, with the creation of the National Park Service (NPS), the site became a national park. Every year, 1.5 million people visit Gettysburg National Military Park to explore the historic battlefield and learn about what happened there in 1863.[24]

Edward Everett

During the time of the American Civil War, Edward Everett was a very popular public speaker. This was why he was chosen to speak before Lincoln at the Gettysburg cemetery dedication. Everett used no notes and spoke for two hours, detailing the battle. He also predicted that the North and South would reunite, once again forming a union. Later, some people criticized Lincoln for his brief speech. But Everett wrote to the president, saying, "I should be glad if I could flatter myself that I came as near to the central idea of the occasion, in two hours, as you did in two minutes."[25]

CHAPTER
TWO

THE VISITOR CENTER AND MUSEUM

Many people begin their visit to Gettysburg National Military Park by going to the Visitor Center and the Gettysburg Museum of the American Civil War. It usually takes four to six hours to experience the entire park.[1] The Visitor Center offers a great introduction to what guests will see at the site.

Guests can stop by the Visitor Center's NPS information desk to pick up a battlefield map and a guidebook. Different versions of the guidebook are printed for spring, summer, and fall. This way, visitors always know what seasonal activities are taking place in the park during their visit. The information desk is also where visitors pay to enter the museum and see exhibits located in the Visitor Center.

In addition to exhibits and information desks, the Gettysburg National Military Park Museum & Visitor Center is home to a bookstore, a café, and a research room.

The Battle of Gettysburg Cyclorama painting depicts Pickett's Charge, which happened on the third day of the battle. Dramatic lighting and sound effects help bring the scene to life for viewers.

Movie and Cyclorama

At the Visitor Center, guests can see the movie *A New Birth of Freedom*. This 20-minute film is narrated by actor Morgan Freeman.[2] It discusses how the Battle of Gettysburg unfolded and why it was important. The film is optional but serves as a good introduction to the battle.

The Visitor Center is also home to the Battle of Gettysburg Cyclorama painting. This is not only an introduction to the battle but also a piece of history itself. In the 1800s, cycloramas were a popular form of entertainment. At the time, people didn't have televisions or movies, and photographs were rare. Cycloramas were huge paintings designed to give viewers an immersive,

360-degree experience. They were often displayed in special auditoriums around a viewing platform.

At the Visitor Center, guests can experience a cyclorama in the same way that people in the 1800s did. A round viewing platform sits in the middle of an octagonal theater. The cyclorama painting encircles this platform behind a physical set or arrangement of props, which includes soil, fence rails, sod, and battle debris. This foreground helps make viewers feel as though they're inside the painting, standing on a battlefield.

In 1882, painter Paul Philippoteaux spent three months on the Gettysburg battlefield researching the landscape.[3] He paid a local photographer to take photos of the battlefield while standing on a raised platform. Back in his studio, Philippoteaux worked with a team of painters to create the massive painting. Each painter had

Gettysburg Cycloramas

At least three Gettysburg cyclorama paintings were created, but only the one at Gettysburg National Military Park is still in good condition.[4] The first cyclorama was painted for display in Chicago, Illinois. After the cyclorama theater there closed, someone eventually bought the painting and later donated it to Wake Forest University in Winston-Salem, North Carolina. The cyclorama currently displayed at Gettysburg was the second one to be painted. A third cyclorama was originally displayed in Denver, Colorado. But it was cut up so the canvas could be used for tents on the Shoshone Reservation.

a specialty. One might paint the landscape while another painted horses. Another might paint the faces of famous people. The artists completed the painting in 1884. It is 42 feet (12.8 m) tall and 377 feet (115 m) long.[5]

The Battle of Gettysburg Cyclorama hasn't always been in Gettysburg. It arrived there in 1962 after being displayed in Boston, Massachusetts. When the painting arrived in Gettysburg, areas of water damage from where the canvas had been in direct contact with the soil of the foreground had to be repaired. Several tears and areas where sunlight had faded the surface were also repaired. This restoration work has helped preserve the cyclorama for today's visitors.

Look Up!

When visitors tour the Gettysburg Museum of the American Civil War, they should remember to look up. Overhead, they will see the beams that once supported the floor of the John Forney farmhouse. This house was located near the northern end of the battlefield in an area where there was heavy fighting on July 1, 1863. An artillery shell passed through the home's floor joists. These horizontal wooden beams are part of the floorboards. Although the home is no longer standing, the joists and the artillery shell fragments are displayed in the museum.

Museum of the American Civil War

Another highlight of the Visitor Center is the museum. It is home to 1.2 million artifacts.[6] Many exhibits in the museum detail the personal, individual lives of soldiers, giving visitors a new perspective of the battle. They showcase artifacts from soldiers' daily lives. These items range from toothbrushes and lice combs to boots and a Bible left behind by retreating Confederates.

Other exhibits explore what life as a soldier was like. One shows what a soldier might eat. Another shows how the cavalry was equipped. The exhibit includes a life-size mannequin of a horse and rider. Guests can also see signal flags, binoculars, and a canteen. One wall displays buttons and belt buckles used by the regiments that fought at Gettysburg, representing the many men who converged on the town. Another display shows different firearms, including pistols and muskets, that were used in the war.

At the Gettysburg Museum of the American Civil War, visitors can see Civil War–era weapons such as cannons. They can also enjoy numerous videos and interactive displays.

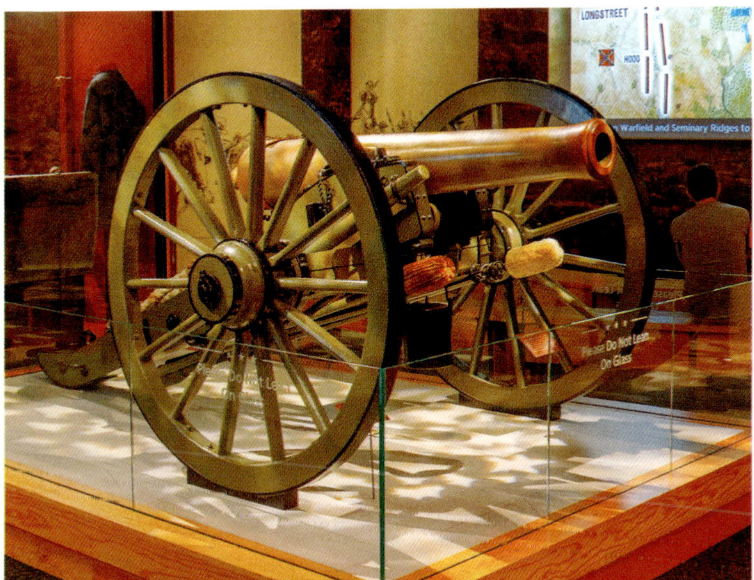

During the American Civil War, Union soldiers wore blue uniforms while Confederate soldiers often wore gray or brownish ones. At Gettysburg, visitors can see military jackets and caps.

The museum also tells the stories of American Civil War soldiers by featuring their photographs and their own words whenever possible. Markers for well-known clashes at the Battle of Gettysburg include photos of real soldiers and letters they wrote to their loved ones. These letters demonstrate that different soldiers fought for different reasons. For example, they may have fought for a home, a sweetheart, a way of life, or a strong conviction. They were individual men with their own hopes and their own reasons for fighting.

The museum doesn't ignore the soldiers of the Confederacy, either. One exhibit includes mannequins outfitted in Confederate uniforms. It features Robert E. Lee's camp setup, which includes his camp bed and travel desk. Visitors can also see the stretcher used to carry the injured Confederate general Stonewall Jackson away from the battle. They can even see the table Jackson was on when his arm was later amputated.

Experiencing History

Touring the museum is not the only way visitors can experience history at the Visitor Center. Rangers who work at the park offer a wide array of programs, including the Junior Ranger Program. To complete this program, young learners complete activities to earn points. The number of points they must earn varies based on their age. Participants can earn points by answering questions, completing puzzles, designing their own tour, or describing a ranger activity. Kids ages 6 to 13 can earn a certificate and a badge.

> **"Learning about the Civil War is a lot of fun, even though being a Civil War soldier was not necessarily very fun.[8]"**
>
> ***—Zach Siggins, park ranger at Gettysburg National Military Park***

Visitors can also go on hikes with park rangers. The Gettysburg History Hike is 90 minutes long and covers sites from all three days of the battle.[7] This includes the Bloody Angle, which was part of Pickett's Charge on the final day of the battle. The Little Round

Don't Miss It!

The Sachs Covered Bridge

The Sachs Covered Bridge is located off Pumping Station Road in Gettysburg. This lattice-truss bridge is 100 feet (30 m) long and was built in 1852 by David Stoner.[9] It crosses over Marsh Creek. During the Battle of Gettysburg, the bridge was used by both the Union and Confederate armies.

According to one story about the bridge, three Confederate soldiers disguised themselves in Union uniforms and tried to flee the area. But Union soldiers realized the men were Confederates. They hanged the Confederate men from the bridge's support beams and left them as a warning to other Confederates. A field hospital was also located near the bridge. Many Confederate soldiers are believed to have died along the creek.

After the war, people continued to use the Sachs Covered Bridge to cross Marsh Creek. They crossed in horse-drawn wagons and later in cars. In 1938, after many other covered bridges had collapsed, the Pennsylvania Department of Highways named the Sachs Covered Bridge Pennsylvania's most historic bridge. In May 1968, the bridge was closed to car traffic to limit the stress on the historic structure.

It's Closed!

With so much to see in the Gettysburg area, it is not always possible to make it to the park when the Visitor Center is open. However, visitors can still tour the park and learn about the battle when the Visitor Center is closed. A nearby kiosk provides park maps and brochures. Guests can also find information about a self-guided online audio tour. Specific dates and times when the Visitor Center will be closed are listed on the park's website. The website includes a schedule with reminders about how the hours of operation vary seasonally.

Top Hike is only an hour long.[10] It offers participants an opportunity to explore the hill's rocky summit and learn why this location was important to both the Union and the Confederacy.

Living history programs are also available. These give visitors an opportunity to walk among costumed re-enactors camped on the battlefield and learn about the tactics, weapons, and tools used by both armies. Guests can learn more about these opportunities by checking the park's online calendar or guidebooks at the Visitor Center desk.

Another way to experience the park is by taking a guided tour. Visitors can pay to take a tour with a licensed guide who has been trained by park officials. Options include car tours and bus tours. Guests can also purchase an audio tour at the park's bookshop or go on the self-guided driving tour, which follows a route marked on the map provided at the Visitor Center desk.

CHAPTER THREE

THE BATTLEFIELD

Because the Gettysburg battlefield encompasses 5,700 acres (2,307 ha), one of the best ways to explore it is to take the NPS's self-guided Auto Tour.[1] This tour highlights important areas of the battlefield. Although visitors can buy tours from various organizations, the Auto Tour can be accessed and purchased online at the park's website. Auto Tour guidebooks and maps are also available at the Visitor Center or the kiosk.

The tour leads visitors through a series of 16 numbered stops. Fifteen of these stops highlight important places on the battlefield, while the sixteenth stop is the National Cemetery.[2] At each stop, visitors can get out of their cars to explore on foot before proceeding to the next stop.

The Auto Tour route at Gettysburg National Military Park is marked by red-and-black signs, which have a white star in the middle. Signs marking Auto Tour stops include numbers.

While exploring the battlefield, visitors can see many monuments. The NPS reports that the battlefield has 1,328 monuments in total, which makes it impossible to see every monument in one trip.[3] Instead, visitors may want to look for examples of all four monument types. Markers and tablets are the first type. The US War Department installed these to mark the locations of officer headquarters—indicated by an upright cannon tube—and troop movements. There are more than 350 markers and tablets in the park.[4]

A second monument type, regimental monuments, are positioned wherever a particular regiment entered the battle. The third monument type is the state monument. State monuments honor soldiers from a specific state who fought at Gettysburg. Each state that had men in the battle has one monument, unless there were men from that state fighting for both the Union and the Confederacy, in which case there are sometimes two.[5]

Overnight Stays

The NPS leases two homes on the Gettysburg battlefield grounds to visitors who want to stay overnight. The two-story Bushman House, built of stone and brick, was the location from which Confederate general John Bell Hood staged his July 2 attack at Devil's Den and Little Round Top.[6] The Slyder House is positioned at the base of Big Round Top. During the battle, Union sharpshooters used the home's stone walls and farm fences as cover while they targeted Confederate forces.

The final monument type is the individual memorial, or a monument dedicated to a single soldier. Most individual memorials at Gettysburg are dedicated to officers. Not every monument with a picture of a soldier on it is an individual monument, because that was a common style for regimental monuments as well. Many of these monuments can be seen at the Auto Tour stops.

Auto Tour Stops

The first stop on the Auto Tour has two areas, 1A and 1B.[7] Both are on McPherson Ridge. From Stop 1A, visitors

A monument to Major General John Buford stands near the first Auto Tour stop. Behind it is a monument to Union general John F. Reynolds, who was killed on the first day of the battle.

can see mountains in the distance. Robert E. Lee was on the far side of these mountains when he learned about the Union Army's proximity. He then ordered his forces to converge on Gettysburg.

General John Buford, commander of the Union cavalry, reached the area on June 30 to defend the town. His men were outnumbered but had carbines, which fired faster than Confederate muskets. On July 1, Buford's men took position along a ridge and fought the Confederates, falling back when ordered. They did this again and again, delaying the Confederates. This gave the rest of the Union forces time to secure a strategic position.

The base of the Eternal Light Peace Memorial is inscribed with the words "Peace Eternal in a Nation United." Two quotes from President Lincoln are inscribed on the monument's sides.

At Stop 1B, visitors can see several monuments. One honors Union general James Samuel Wadsworth. The statue depicts Wadsworth pointing into the distance. There are also several regimental monuments, including the 147th New York Infantry Monument and the Ninety-fifth New York Infantry Monument. Both of these monuments are topped with polished stone spheres.

The second tour stop is the Eternal Light Peace Memorial on Oak Hill. Confederate troops led by Major General Robert E. Rodes attacked from the hill on which this monument stands. They moved against the Union forces on McPherson Ridge and Oak Ridge to drive the Union Army back to Gettysburg. However, Rodes's troops failed because of poorly coordinated attacks.

The Eternal Light Peace Memorial is a stone platform with an eternal flame burning atop a rectangular pillar. It is built out of granite from northern Maine and limestone from southern Alabama, representing the North and the South. President Franklin Delano Roosevelt dedicated the memorial on July 3, 1938. More than 1,000 Civil War veterans, many of whom were more than 90 years old at the time, attended the ceremony.[8]

For Stop 3, visitors move to Oak Ridge, where Union forces were stationed to defend three major roads.

The stop faces the Confederate line on Oak Hill, which can easily be seen from an observation deck. Union forces, driven from this point through the town, regrouped on Cemetery Hill south of town.

The fourth stop features the North Carolina Memorial. It is located on Seminary Ridge along West Confederate Avenue. This road did not exist at the time of the battle but was added later to accommodate visitors. As visitors travel down the road, they see cannons pointing toward Cemetery Ridge where the Union forces gathered. These cannons mark where Confederate artillery batteries were positioned for battle on July 2.

Stop 5 is the Virginia State Memorial. It marks the position from which Robert E. Lee watched Pickett's Charge. Visitors can see much of what Lee would have seen during the battle—an open field with little cover for his advancing army. Still, on July 3, Lee ordered his men to advance. The Virginia State Memorial is the largest Confederate monument on the Auto Tour. At the base of the column are statues of seven Virginia soldiers.[9] A statue of Lee on a horse sits atop a square granite column.

Stop 6 is called Pitzer Woods. On the second day of the battle, Confederate general James Longstreet and his men had to reach this position without being seen

Don't Miss It!

Little Round Top

Little Round Top is the eighth stop on the Auto Tour. During the Battle of Gettysburg, it was a critical point in the Union line. But it was left undefended because General Daniel Sickles didn't like the rocky ground or the trees blocking his view there. He had moved his men to the Peach Orchard instead. This left a gap in the Union line, leaving it vulnerable to attacks. When Meade heard about this hole, he dispatched troops to fill it. The Union troops raced to get to Little Round Top before the advancing Confederates did.

Little Round Top is one of the most popular spots on the Auto Tour. This is because of the view it provides of the surrounding battlefield. Three paved paths lead to the top of Little Round Top.[10] Along the paths, visitors can see various wayside exhibits that provide information about the battle.

There are also numerous monuments at Little Round Top. The monument for the Twelfth and Forty-fourth New York Infantry Regiments looks like a castle. It is the largest regimental monument in the park. The Ninety-first Pennsylvania Infantry Monument is a granite tower that stands over 25 feet (8 m) tall.[11] The tower is topped with a Maltese cross.

Hundreds of cannons are placed throughout the Gettysburg battlefield. At the Peach Orchard, two cannons flank a monument dedicated to Battery F, Pennsylvania Light Artillery.

by Union troops in order to carry out Lee's battle plan. This meant Longstreet sometimes had to double back and didn't get to Pitzer Woods until 3:00 p.m. At this stop, visitors can gaze across the battlefield from the Longstreet Observation Tower.

Stop 7 is on Warfield Ridge, where Alabama troops gathered prior to the battle. From this spot, visitors can see Stop 8, Little Round Top, to the left. They can also see Big Round Top to the right. Despite its higher elevation, Big Round Top was too heavily forested to be a defensible position during the battle, while Little Round Top was not. Visitors at Stop 7 can also see several memorials. One is the Alabama State Memorial. It depicts a woman, the Spirit of the Confederacy, urging two men to keep fighting. The other memorial is the Confederate Soldiers and Sailors Memorial, which depicts a color bearer urging his comrades forward.

Stop 9 is the Wheatfield, a 26-acre (10.5 ha) field that sat at the center of a two-and-a-half-hour clash on July 2. During this clash, the field changed hands six times until the Union was eventually driven back to Cemetery Ridge. After this battle, more than 4,000 men lay dead or wounded.[12] Today, paths through the Wheatfield lead visitors to various state monuments. These include the Twenty-seventh Connecticut Infantry Monument, which is topped with an eagle, and the First New York Light Artillery Monument, which has a polished orb on top.

The next stop on the tour is the Peach Orchard, which was owned by Joseph Sherfy at the time of the battle. Union major general Daniel Sickles positioned his men at

Signal Flags

During the American Civil War, armies communicated over long distances using signal flags. These came in three sizes: 2 by 2 feet (0.6 by 0.6 m), 4 by 4 feet (1.2 by 1.2 m), and 6 by 6 feet (1.8 by 1.8 m). The smallest flag was used when men had to lie down or signal while in protective cover. The largest flag was visible from 15 miles (24 km) away.[13] Flags came in different colors, including white with a red center and red or black with a white center. Signal men chose flags based on which colors would be most visible.

this orchard because he liked its landscape better than the landscape of Little Round Top, where Meade had ordered him to go. But the group's position at the orchard placed the men ahead of the rest of the Union line, leaving part of the line undefended. Sickles's men were decimated and unfit for further duty after July 2. Today, visitors at the stop can see Sherfy's family home, which is still riddled with bullet holes from the battle.

> **General Trimble of the Confederate Army, was [today] found wounded just outside of Gettysburg. Gen. Hemper was found mortally wounded on the road to Fairfield, and a large number of wounded estimated at several thousand.**[15]
>
> ***—General George Gordon Meade, in a letter to General Henry Halleck in Washington, DC, July 6, 1863***

Tour Stop 11 is Plum Run. This is a creek along which Union troops retreated to Cemetery Ridge, which is a quarter of a mile (0.4 km) away. Cemetery Ridge is Tour Stop 12. The ridge is only 30 to 40 feet (9–12 m) higher than the valley below it, but it gave the Union troops an advantage.[14] Today, cannons and monuments placed along the ridge indicate where Union troops were positioned to fend off the Confederates.

Visitors can climb a spiral staircase to the top of the Pennsylvania State Memorial, which stands 110 feet

(34 m) tall. The names of 34,530 Pennsylvania men who fought at Gettysburg appear on bronze plaques around the structure, with stars indicating the fallen.[16] The memorial is the tallest state monument at Gettysburg.

Spangler's Spring is Stop 13 on the tour. It is named after a natural freshwater spring located at the site. On the evening of the first day of fighting, the Union Army stacked stones to create a defensive line above the spring. On the second day, they were outnumbered but

A bronze statue of a woman holding a sword stands at the top of the Pennsylvania State Memorial. The winged figure, who represents Victory, is made of metal from melted cannons.

Visitors can't go inside the Lydia Leister House, but they can stand on the home's front porch and look through its windows to see two rooms.

held strong. It took seven hours of fighting the next day to drive the Confederates back.[17]

Tour Stop 14 is called East Cemetery Hill but is located on Stevens Knoll. At this stop, visitors can stand behind a split-rail fence to see Cemetery Hill. This critical position was narrowly held by the Union throughout the Battle of Gettysburg.

Stop 15 is called the High Water Mark. It is the site of Pickett's Charge, the final decisive clash of the battle. Visitors can see the open ground over which Lee's men advanced. At the High Water Mark—the farthest point up the ridge reached by Confederate troops—stands a monument dedicated to all the troops. It features a bronze statue shaped like an open book. It names the divisions and brigades from both armies that fought at Gettysburg.

Lydia Leister House

Aside from the Auto Tour stops, guests can see other important places on the battlefield. Lydia Leister's home is one of the farmhouses on the field. Leister was a widow. Before the battle, she and her two daughters fled the home. General Meade used the house as his headquarters.

As the Confederates shelled Cemetery Ridge, shells passed over the hill and struck the house and farmyard. Horses in the yard were killed. Another shell passed through the house's garret, or attic. Meade evacuated and set up headquarters in a new area.

Today, people can visit the Lydia Leister House. They can see how a typical home would have been furnished at the time of the war. The surviving furniture from the home is displayed in the Gettysburg Museum of the American Civil War. Reproductions of the furniture are displayed in the home itself.

Damage at Leister Farm

When Lydia Leister returned to her farm after the Battle of Gettysburg, she discovered 17 dead horses in the yard. Her livestock was missing. Her peach trees, apple trees, and wheat were all destroyed. Leister told a reporter that she received no compensation from the government for her damaged property. However, she did sell the bones of the dead horses at 50 cents per pound. Leister replanted her crops and thrived, buying more land and adding a two-story addition to the house.[18]

CHAPTER
FOUR

NATIONAL CEMETERY

During and after the Battle of Gettysburg, dead soldiers were buried as quickly as possible. But because there were so many men to bury, the original burials were often shallow graves. Some had stones or turf on top to keep animals from digging up the bodies.

Survivors didn't have time to create elaborate markers for the graves, so if there was any marker at all, it was often a simple headboard. The rectangular wooden boards might have a soldier's name or regiment carved or written on them. These simple graves were generally for Union soldiers. Confederate soldiers were often interred in mass graves.

However, the graves did not stay in good condition. Loose soil can easily be

The New York State Monument stands near the New York section of Soldiers' National Cemetery. It includes the names of New York officers who died or were fatally wounded during the Battle of Gettysburg.

washed away by rain. Because the original burials at Gettysburg were shallow, rain sometimes exposed the feet and legs of the deceased. This made the remains easy for animals to reach. Sometimes people spotted hogs running away from burial grounds carrying limbs.

Pennsylvania governor Andrew Curtin visited Gettysburg one week after the battle. He saw the

In Soldiers' National Cemetery, sections are marked with rectangular gray stones that list the number of fallen soldiers within that section. Marble squares serve as graves for unknown soldiers.

deteriorating headboards around the field. Curtin realized that if the graves were not updated, they would soon become so worn that no one would know who was buried in which grave. He believed the soldiers who had given their lives in the battle deserved more honorable burials. To accomplish this, a cemetery needed to be created.

When local attorney David Wills sent Curtin a proposal to establish a cemetery for the men who had died at Gettysburg, Curtin approved it. He also appointed Wills to the position of Pennsylvania state agent. This meant Wills had the authority to purchase land and arrange new burials for Pennsylvanians who had died in the battle. Governors of other states supported the project too. Agents representing New York, Ohio, Indiana, Connecticut, and Massachusetts arrived in Gettysburg to oversee the burial of deceased soldiers from their states.

Designing the Cemetery

Landscape architect William Saunders designed the Gettysburg cemetery. His vision was to create a cemetery that was simple, elegant, and easy to maintain. He recommended placing a monument at the highest point of a hill. Burials would be arranged in a half circle around the monument. The half circle would be sectioned so that each of the 18 participating states had a wedge-shaped portion stretching from the center.[1]

Because of the half-circle format, the graves at this cemetery are equally spaced around parallel semicircular arcs. Each grave is allotted seven feet (2 m) of space, with no distinction between military ranking or between states.[2] As visitors gaze across the cemetery, it is easy to see these semicircles extending outward from the monument.

Before soldiers could be buried in the cemetery, they had to be disinterred from their original burial places and moved. Wills hired Samuel Weaver to oversee this process. A crew of approximately 12 free Black men worked under the direction of Basil Biggs to do the digging.[3] Bodies were placed in wooden coffins. All personal belongings that had been buried with the soldiers were cataloged and

Major General John F. Reynolds

Union major general John F. Reynolds is not buried in Gettysburg. But the first bronze statue erected at Gettysburg is a monument that honors him. Dedicated in 1872, it depicts Reynolds standing in full uniform. The statue was made using metal from four cannons. Reynolds was the highest-ranking man killed during the battle, and the men he commanded commissioned the statue. The park also includes two other monuments for Reynolds.[4] One is a stone marker at the spot where he was killed. The other is a statue of the general on his horse. It is located on Chambersburg Pike.

The Lincoln Address Memorial is located at the south end of Gettysburg National Cemetery, near the Taneytown Road entrance. The monument was dedicated in January 1912.

stored so that they could be given to family members who might ask for them.

The task of reburying the dead started in August, when the weather was warm and humid. The decomposing bodies smelled, and Wills worried that the bodies might spread diseases when the workers dug them up. Because of this, the job was postponed until October, when the weather was cooler. All reburials were finally completed on March 18, 1864.

Today, visitors to the cemetery can view the graves of all 3,500 Union soldiers interred there, including 979 unidentified men.[5] Sometimes workers could tell which state a soldier was from by his uniform. These men were buried in the appropriate state section. Their markers read "unknown." If workers didn't know a soldier's name or state, he was buried wherever there was an unclaimed grave and given a numbered marker. Even unidentifiable soldiers were given a place in the cemetery.

The Gettysburg Address

The cemetery was dedicated on November 19, 1863. On this day, Lincoln delivered his Gettysburg Address. Near the entrance to the cemetery, visitors can see the Lincoln Address Memorial. It features a curved stone wall with a bust of Lincoln at the center. Sculptor Henry Bush-Brown created the bust of Lincoln, which has a deeply lined face and downcast eyes.

To the left of the sculpture is a plaque with the text of the letter Wills sent to invite Lincoln to the dedication. To the right is a plaque with the text of the speech itself. Many visitors believe the monument was built in the place Lincoln stood while delivering the speech, but that is not the case. Historians disagree about exactly where Lincoln might have stood during the Gettysburg Address.

Near the monument is a metal marker that says, "The Address was delivered about 300 yards [274 m] from

An Iconic Speech

In the Gettysburg Address, Lincoln referred back to the founding of the United States. He drew a line between the nation's original promise of freedom and the struggles it was facing during the war. "Four score and seven years ago our fathers brought forth on this continent a new nation, conceived in liberty, and dedicated to the proposition that all men are created equal," Lincoln said. "Now we are engaged in a great civil war, testing whether that nation . . . can long endure."[7] The war didn't end until two years after Lincoln gave his speech. But today, many people consider it to be one of the greatest US speeches of all time. Lines from the speech are inscribed on the walls of the Lincoln Memorial in Washington, DC.

this spot along the Upper Cemetery Drive. The site is now marked by the Soldiers' National Monument."[6] This is not where Lincoln stood during the speech, but many people once believed it was.

Another structure that people mistakenly think is the spot where Lincoln delivered the Gettysburg Address is the Rostrum. This is a brick speaker's stand, or a platform sheltered under a slatted, pergola-style roof. Historic photos of this structure label it as the rostrum from which Lincoln spoke.

However, it was constructed to the right of the cemetery entrance in 1879, 16 years after the Gettysburg Address was delivered. Lincoln never used the Rostrum. But several other US presidents, including Franklin Delano Roosevelt in 1934 and Dwight D. Eisenhower in 1955, have stood on the platform to deliver speeches.

The figure of Liberty on top of Soldiers' National Monument holds a sword and a laurel wreath in her hands. The monument includes an inscription of words from the Gettysburg Address.

Visitors who want to know where Lincoln stood during the Gettysburg Address won't find a memorial marking the precise location. However, it was calculated in 2024 by Christopher Oakley, an associate professor at the University of North Carolina Asheville. Oakley's students were creating a digital animation of Lincoln's speech, and he wanted to provide them an accurate background.

Oakley studied several historic photos and used a graphics program to discover that the many people involved in the ceremony sat on a large trapezoidal platform. It straddled the boundary between Evergreen Cemetery and Soldiers' National Cemetery. The speakers, including Lincoln, stood in the National Cemetery.

Visitors at the cemetery can see a second memorial dedicated to Lincoln too. The Kentucky Memorial was installed in 1975 to honor Lincoln, who was born in Kentucky. The memorial looks like the top of a stone speaker's podium and includes bronze tablets containing the text of the Gettysburg Address.

> **We see the symbolic story of American peace and plenty living under freedom following a heroic struggle among its own people.**[8]
>
> ***—Dave Stotts, host of the show* Drive Thru History*, on the Soldiers' National Monument***

Soldiers' National Monument

Visitors are sure to spot the Soldiers' National Monument sitting atop the hill in the National Cemetery. It is at the highest point on the hill, as recommended by Saunders. Although the cornerstone was laid on July 4, 1865, the full monument was not completed until 1869. It was dedicated on July 1, 1869, marking the completion of the cemetery.

The Soldiers' National Monument honors the men who fell during the Battle of Gettysburg. It was sculpted by Randolph Rogers, who put four figures around the base of the statue. One is a soldier, who represents War. The second is Clio, the Greek muse of history. She is depicted as a woman writing on a tablet. The third figure is a woman holding wheat, who represents Plenty, and the fourth is a mechanic, who represents Peace. The figure of Liberty at the top makes the monument 60 feet (18 m) tall. Around the column are 18 bronze stars representing the 18 states whose soldiers fought in the Union Army.[9]

General Meade spoke at the dedication of the memorial. In his speech, Meade praised the men who were buried in the cemetery. But he also called for his listeners to do something about the many Confederate soldiers who had been buried in shallow battlefield graves or alongside temporary hospitals. Meade stated that even the fallen enemy should be buried with decency and respect.

Weaver began the task of disinterring the Confederate dead, identifying them whenever possible. When he was killed in an 1871 railroad accident, the task fell to his son, Rufus Weaver. Between 1871 and 1873, the younger Weaver shipped 3,320 Confederate remains to Richmond, Virginia; Raleigh, North Carolina; Charleston, South Carolina; and Savannah, Georgia.[10]

Friend to Friend Masonic Memorial

Friend to Friend Masonic Memorial is in Gettysburg National Cemetery. It was dedicated in 1993 and depicts Union Army captain Henry H. Bingham assisting wounded Confederate brigadier general Lewis Armistead after Pickett's Charge. The two men were Freemasons, or members of an international organization that encourages people to befriend and help each other. The group holds elaborate ceremonies that only members are allowed to attend. A popular story about the Battle of Gettysburg is that when Armistead was wounded, he gave a Masonic hand sign. Bingham saw the sign and hurried over to assist his fellow Freemason.

Later Burials

The National Cemetery has expanded since the soldiers from the Battle of Gettysburg were buried there. The Civil War section is called Soldiers' National Cemetery, but the entire cemetery is known as Gettysburg National Cemetery. Within this larger cemetery is a section known as the annex, which is located north of Soldiers' National Cemetery.

In the annex, visitors see headstones arranged in rows, which is traditional in most military cemeteries. This expansion was originally added so veterans of the Spanish-American War (1898) could be interred in

While graves in Soldiers' National Cemetery are marked with flat, ground-level stones, graves in the annex are marked with traditional headstones.

the cemetery. The annex also includes burials of veterans who fought in World War I (1914–1918), World War II (1939–1945), the Korean War (1950–1953), and the Vietnam War (1955–1975).

Burials in the annex were suspended in the 1960s until 17 more acres (7 ha) were added in 1968. This made

space for another 1,700 graves of veterans and their spouses.[11] When the annex reached capacity again, the cemetery officially closed to new burials, except for spouses, in 1978. The only veteran's burial since then occurred in 1997, when the grave of an American Civil War soldier was found on Seminary Ridge.

CHAPTER
FIVE

HISTORICAL SITES IN GETTYSBURG

Outside of the battlefield, visitors can enjoy many historical sites and experiences in Gettysburg. One site is the Gettysburg Lincoln Railroad Station. On November 2, 1863, David Wills invited Lincoln to travel to Gettysburg for the National Cemetery dedication.

The distance between Washington, DC, and Gettysburg is about 81 miles (130 km). Today, visitors traveling between the two cities can make the journey by car in about an hour and a half, but it was not as simple in 1863.[1] Travelers could walk, ride a horse, ride in a wagon or carriage, or take a train.

At noon on November 17, Lincoln, three of his cabinet members, and at least 50 guards and military members boarded a train with four passenger cars to make

The Gettysburg Lincoln Railroad Station is located at 35 Carlisle Street. Before and during the Battle of Gettysburg, the station served as the town's first field hospital.

During the American Civil War, Cornelia Hancock cared for soldiers wounded in many major battles. She can be seen in an 1863 photograph of Brandy Station field hospital in Virginia.

the journey to Gettysburg.[2] At that time, there was no direct train line to Gettysburg from Washington, DC. In Baltimore, Maryland, the train stopped at one station and the locomotive was detached. Then teams of horses pulled the passenger cars to another station in Baltimore, where the cars were attached to a different locomotive to continue the journey.

As the train neared Gettysburg, the travelers experienced other delays because the track and the railbed on which the track was laid were in bad condition. Because of the war, no maintenance had been done on the tracks. Nevertheless, Lincoln arrived in Gettysburg late in the evening on November 17 at what is now known as the Gettysburg Lincoln Railroad Station.

Virtual Gettysburg

Today, Gettysburg Lincoln Railroad Station offers visitors the opportunity to see Gettysburg as it looked in 1863. This is made possible using modern virtual reality (VR) technology. The VR experience is called Ticket to the Past. Visitors pay a fee to use a VR headset. It allows them to follow one of three Gettysburg residents.[3]

> **"It was pleasant to see [Lincoln's] sad face lighted up. He was looking very badly at that particular time, being sallow, sunken-eyed, thin, care-worn and very quiet.[4]"**
>
> ***—Lieutenant Henry Clay Cochrane, describing Lincoln on the 1863 train journey to Gettysburg***

One historical figure whom guests can choose to follow in the VR experience is Cornelia Hancock, a soldier caregiver. At a time when young women did not normally travel alone, 23-year-old Hancock defied convention and traveled to the battlefield from Philadelphia, Pennsylvania. In Gettysburg, she served as a volunteer nurse.

Another choice is Eli Blanchard, an 18-year-old Iron Brigade soldier. The Iron Brigade was composed of infantry and light artillery men who were primarily from Wisconsin. Visitors who choose Blanchard, a volunteer soldier, accompany him first as an Iron Brigade drummer and then as a surgeon's assistant working in a makeshift hospital.

The third person whom visitors can choose is Basil Biggs, a free Black man. Visitors follow Biggs as he journeys to the train station after the Battle of Gettysburg to collect supplies needed to exhume bodies. Biggs played a vital role in reburying fallen soldiers in the National Cemetery and in returning their possessions to loved ones.

Expanding and Growing the Park

Periodically, land is added to Gettysburg National Military Park. In 2011, part of the Harman farm, which had later been made into a golf course, was donated to the park. In 2014, Congress voted to expand the park's boundary to include the Gettysburg Lincoln Railroad Station within the town of Gettysburg. These additions make it easier for the NPS to preserve the historic properties and sometimes restore them to how they appeared in 1863.

The David Wills House

Another notable site is the David Wills House. Wills, who facilitated the formation of the cemetery and invited Lincoln to speak at its dedication, had a home located at the center of the battle. When Confederate soldiers came into town looking for supplies on June 26, 1863, Wills gathered people together to hide in his home's basement. Like many other buildings in town, Wills's home was filled with wounded and dying soldiers, along with

The David Wills House opened as a museum on February 12, 2009, to celebrate President Lincoln's 200th birthday. Today, the town square in which the home stands is called Lincoln Square.

local women working as nurses. When the US Sanitary Commission arrived in Gettysburg, it used Wills's home as a temporary warehouse to store supplies. Gettysburg citizens also met at the home to make plans for the cemetery. Today, the house is a museum.

When Lincoln arrived in Gettysburg, he was brought to Wills's home to spend the night. Wills and his wife, Catherine, also hosted several other distinguished guests. While exploring the museum, visitors can learn more about this and view the bedroom where Lincoln put the final touches on the Gettysburg Address.

The first gallery in the museum is the *Wills Parlor*. Instead of being set up like a typical 1800s parlor, the room contains a diorama of Gettysburg as it appeared at the time of the battle. The room also includes displays about what occurred during the battle. Adjoining the parlor is Wills's law office, which is set up as it would have appeared in 1863 with a table, chair, and bookshelves. It contains displays about Wills's role in establishing the cemetery.

In the *Lincoln Bedroom* gallery at the David Wills House, visitors can see the bed that Lincoln slept in the night before he gave the Gettysburg Address.

Visiting the Wills House

It can be tricky to plan a visit to the David Wills House because it is open only at limited times. The free museum is open from spring through early fall, usually from May 11 to November 17. But even during these dates, the house is open only on Fridays, Saturdays, and Sundays from 11:00 a.m. to 4:00 p.m.[6] Visitors who cannot make the trip when the museum is open are encouraged to take advantage of a 3D tour of the house, which is available on the NPS website.

Visitors can see more on the second floor of the David Wills House. Gallery Three is at the top of the stairs and focuses on the Gettysburg Address. Gallery Four focuses on Lincoln's presence in Gettysburg.

At the time, the town was overflowing with people. Many of them were there so they could see the president at the cemetery dedication. When Lincoln arrived at the Wills house, Catherine Wills served dinner to 38 people, including Governor Curtin and Edward Everett.[5]

Gallery Five is the *Lincoln Bedroom*. It contains much of the original furniture that was there when Lincoln spent the night in the room. Gallery Six focuses on the legacy of the Gettysburg Address. Visitors can watch a video and enjoy an interactive display. Gallery Seven is in the hallway. It focuses on what has been done to preserve the historic Wills house.

Following in Lincoln's Footsteps

Visitors who are ready to stretch their legs can follow the route Lincoln took to reach the cemetery and give the Gettysburg Address. Lincoln and other important visitors started in Gettysburg's town square, which is called the Diamond. It is located beside the David Wills House. From the Diamond, they proceeded one mile (1.6 km) to the cemetery.[7] Lincoln rode a horse on the journey, but visitors who walk the route can look for various historical sights along the way.

As visitors walk down Baltimore Street and cross East High Street, they can look to the left and see the current location of the Gettysburg Presbyterian Church. Lincoln visited this church during his time in Gettysburg. On the left side of Baltimore Street, visitors can also see two Witness Trees.[8] These are trees that are old enough to have witnessed critical historic events.

Gettysburg Presbyterian Church

Lincoln left Gettysburg on the same day he gave the Gettysburg Address. But first, he attended what was described as a patriotic meeting at the local Presbyterian church. There, he met local hero John Burns, and the pair spent some time seated together on one of the church pews. The church building that visitors see today was erected in 1963. But the pew in which Lincoln and Burns sat has a plaque on it to make it easy for visitors to find.

A Witness Tree that currently stands along Baltimore Street can be seen on the right side of a photograph of a crowd headed to the cemetery dedication ceremony on November 19, 1863.

The Witness Trees on Baltimore Street are more than 160 years old, making them living links to the Battle of Gettysburg.[9] Lincoln likely passed the trees on his way to the cemetery dedication. Several Witness Trees are scattered across the Gettysburg battlefield grounds. Others, including the ones that visitors pass on their way to the cemetery, are located within the town itself.

Visitors following Lincoln's route can turn onto Steinwehr Avenue, which was called Emmitsburg Road when Lincoln made his journey. Today, people walking the route can use the pedestrian entrance off Steinwehr Avenue to enter the cemetery. Lincoln would have continued down Emmitsburg Road to Taneytown Road to enter.

CHAPTER
SIX

SEMINARY RIDGE MUSEUM

Seminary Ridge was an important part of the Gettysburg battlefield. It is named after the Lutheran Theological Seminary, which still stands on top of the hill. Today, visitors can climb to the cupola on the roof, where they can survey the landscape much as Brigadier General John Buford did after he and his men arrived in Gettysburg on June 30, 1863.

From the cupola, Buford could see Confederate campfires in the distance. Knowing that a battle was coming, Buford used this vantage point to lay out his battle plans so that his troops, despite being outnumbered, could defend the roads. The next morning, Buford's chief signal officer, Lieutenant Aaron Jerome, took up a position in the cupola. Union forces in the

Schmucker Hall is named after Samuel Simon Schmucker, the founder of the Lutheran Theological Seminary. Today, the building houses museum exhibits and a Civil War–themed escape room.

John Buford participated in several major battles of the American Civil War, but he is best known for his leadership during the Battle of Gettysburg. He died of typhoid fever in December 1863.

vicinity were still outnumbered because reinforcements had not yet arrived. But two miles (3 km) away, Jerome saw another force moving toward the battle.[1] He needed to figure out whether it was a Confederate or Union force.

Through his binoculars, Jerome eventually spotted the flag that the men carried and recognized them as Major General John F. Reynolds's forces. Knowing that help was on the way, Buford held out against the Confederates for half an hour until Reynolds was able to reach the battle.[2] Buford's actions might have been different if Jerome had not spotted the advancing Union soldiers.

The Lutheran Seminary

The Lutheran Theological Seminary at Gettysburg was founded in 1826. It is the country's oldest Lutheran seminary. The seminary's location was chosen because it is at a crossroads. This made it easy for students from all over the region to reach the seminary. For its first 30 years, the building was in the quiet countryside beyond the town. But in 1863, it was surrounded by fighting throughout the first day of the Battle of Gettysburg.

As the fighting grew more intense, the injured were moved into Schmucker Hall, the main seminary building with the cupola. Late on the afternoon of July 1, Union forces were pushed out of the area. Schmucker Hall remained under Confederate control until the end of the battle. The building is now a museum known as Seminary Ridge Museum & Education Center.

Fourth Floor

Although it may seem logical to start touring the Seminary Ridge Museum on the first floor, visitors are told to start on the fourth floor. Except for the attic and cupola, all areas of the museum are handicap accessible, and visitors can take either the stairs or the elevator. The gallery on the fourth floor is titled *Gettysburg, July 1, 1863,* and it focuses on the first day of the battle. The museum's galleries are numbered, which makes it easy for visitors to know how to proceed.

Each gallery features large backdrop paintings, photographs, and artifacts. The first gallery is called *We Have Come to Stay!* It includes a nearly life-size photo of Robert E. Lee. Exhibits describe the skirmishes Lee's troops engaged in as they headed north. One backdrop painting shows Gettysburg residents loading a stagecoach and evacuating the town. Artifacts in the gallery space include minié balls and fragmented artillery shells.

The second gallery on the fourth floor is called *Buford's View*. This gallery offers an alternative for visitors who can't take the cupola tour. It displays historic photographs that show the view Buford had from the cupola. The photos are arranged as if visitors are viewing the surrounding area from the cupola. They are labeled with directions such as "View to the Southeast" and "View to the South."

Visitors can also push a button to make key features in the photographs light up. For example, on the "View to the Southeast" photo, pushing the button lights up downtown Gettysburg, Culp's Hill, and Cemetery Ridge. Artifacts in the gallery include a telescope and set of binoculars. Additional galleries on the fourth floor focus

Don't Miss It!

The Cupola Tour

Visitors to Seminary Ridge Museum can pay an extra fee to take the Cupola Tour. The cupola that guests see on this guided tour is not the building's original one. The original burned after being struck by lightning in August 1913. Although the cupola burned, the slate roof of the building and the cupola's metal floor helped keep the fire from spreading. The cupola was later rebuilt to match the original.

Many visitors rate the Cupola Tour as the highlight of their experience at the museum. However, the tour is not handicap accessible, and small children are not allowed. Visitors must climb 50 steps to get to the cupola, so wearing comfortable shoes is recommended. The last step is 18 inches (46 cm) tall and feels like stepping into a bathtub.[3] There are handrails, landings, and an attic that allow people to rest while making the ascent.

Visitors who make the climb can look out from the cupola and get a feel for the distances the battle encompassed. They see the mountains to the west where Buford and Jerome watched for Confederate campfires. This distance is why signal flags, telescopes, and binoculars issued to signal corps members, including Jerome, were important. Visitors can bring their own binoculars for a better view.

on the morning, midday, afternoon, and evening of the first day of the battle.

Third Floor

The third floor of Seminary Ridge Museum focuses on the building's use as a field hospital for both Union and Confederate soldiers. One of the first things visitors see on this floor is a large painting of people aiding the wounded, dressing wounds, and writing letters. There are also enlarged historical photos of hospital tents and wounded men after they had begun to heal. Artifacts on the floor include prosthetic limbs, a stretcher, a surgeon's field case, a tourniquet, a surgeon's amputation kit, and a book about performing various surgeries.

Dr. James Fulton

At the beginning of the American Civil War, there were approximately 55,000 doctors in the United States.[4] However, most were poorly trained. This was partially because students had to travel to Europe to get the best medical education. It was also because the causes of diseases were poorly understood. Dr. James Fulton was a Union Army physician who had professionally trained as a doctor, which was a new idea in medical care at the time. He was sent to Gettysburg to establish a field hospital and was captured by the Confederates. Although Fulton remained a prisoner throughout the battle, he aided patients and dressed their wounds.

Some galleries on the third floor are set up to look like rooms as they would have appeared during the battle. One gallery, *The Wounded*, shows a student's dorm room that has been turned into a hospital room. A realistic mannequin lies in a bed while others sprawl on the floor, sit in chairs, or lean against the wall. Exhibits such as these emphasize that the building is more than a museum. Visitors see things much as they would have looked at the time of the American Civil War.

> **Surgeons are being tested for their abilities and using the carnage of the battle to build knowledge.**[5]
>
> *—Peter Miele, former executive director of Seminary Ridge Museum, describing the gallery* **The Surgeons**

It is important for visitors to understand that because Seminary Ridge was a hospital, some of the displays on the third floor are grim. Artifacts include bones removed from soldiers, some of which still carry bullet fragments. The gallery *The Surgeons* depicts a dorm room set up as an operating theater for amputations. The display includes bloody rags and bandages. At the time of the American Civil War, surgeries were performed with the patient anesthetized with chloroform. Patients breathed in vapors coming from this liquid until they became unconscious.

Other galleries in the museum include stories of hope. One gallery depicts survivors of the battle with their family members, including a wife and two children visiting their husband and father. A desk display also shows that nurses frequently wrote letters on behalf of injured men and mailed them to their families.

Second Floor

The second floor of Seminary Ridge Museum features the gallery *Faith and Freedom in America*. It focuses on the seminary, religious beliefs, and the experience of Black Americans during the American Civil War. One backdrop painting on this floor is a reproduction of Eastman Johnson's 1862 painting *A Ride for Liberty—The Fugitive Slaves*.

In the painting, Johnson depicts a Black father, mother, child, and infant fleeing on horseback as Union and Confederate forces fight in the background. The text that accompanies the painting explains that by 1860, four million enslaved people labored in the United States and its territories.[6] Laws made it illegal to help enslaved people who had run away.

Another gallery is called *Questions of Faith*. Here, visitors can see exhibits that discuss how Christians were

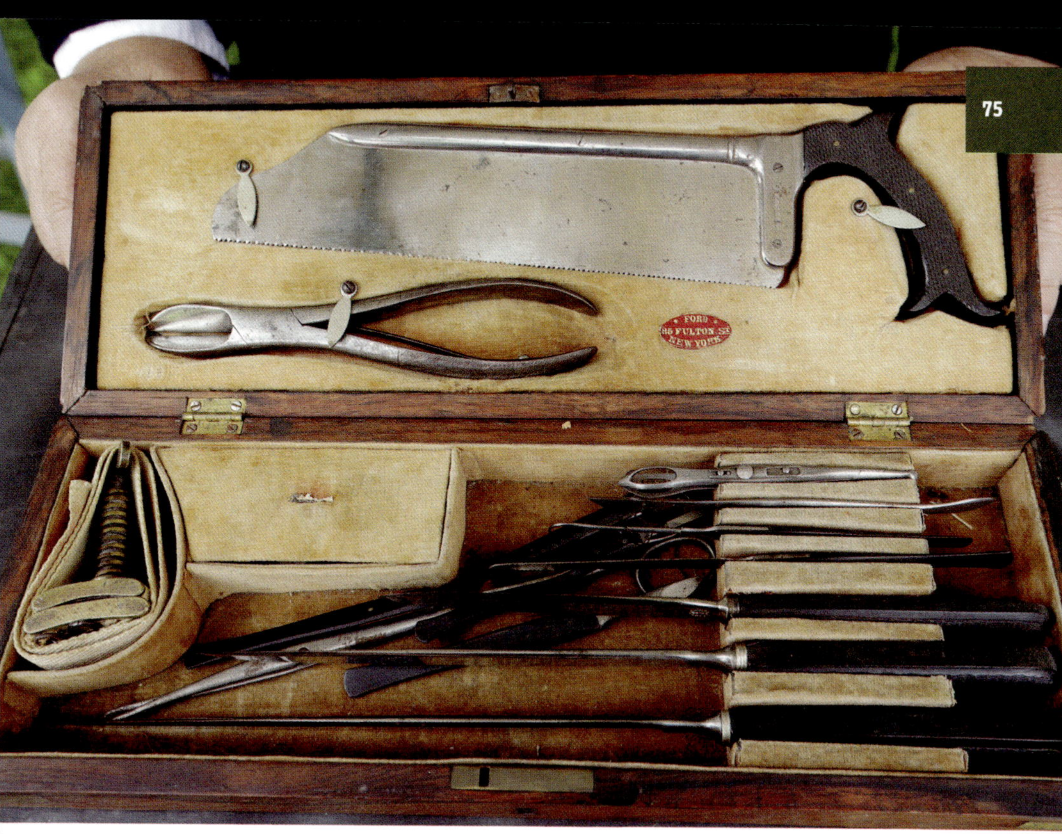

At Seminary Ridge Museum, visitors learn about Civil War–era medical supplies such as amputation kits. These kits contained various scalpels and surgical saws.

divided over the subject of slavery. Some used the Bible to defend slavery, while others used the Bible to condemn the practice. As the nation grew more divided over the issue of slavery, so did some religious denominations. Some even split into Northern and Southern churches.

Although visitors may think it was easy to separate Northern and Southern beliefs, one gallery explains that divisions between free states and slave states were not always clear or easily defined. The gallery is titled *Adams County*. The people who lived in Adams County, which includes Gettysburg, had many business ties with states

Today, the Lutheran Theological Seminary at Gettysburg is called the United Lutheran Seminary. The site includes a chapel called the Church of the Abiding Presence.

that allowed slavery and with people who were enslavers. Because of these ties, people were not always eager to speak out against slavery.

The next gallery is called *African Americans*. It offers information about the Black residents of Gettysburg.

This includes displays about men who joined the Union Army to fight for the freedom of enslaved people in Southern states. Additional displays on the floor explore the antislavery movement.

The final gallery, *The Last Full Measure of Devotion*, focuses on the legacy of the American Civil War. It explores how the states reunited after the war and discusses how exclusion and discrimination have affected the nation. It also considers how people continue to fight for equality today.

The first floor of Seminary Ridge Museum is home to temporary displays that change on a regular basis. Here, visitors can also learn more about touring Robert E. Lee's headquarters. It is managed by the museum's staff and located only a short distance away.

Lee's Headquarters

The home of widow Mary Thompson stands only a quarter of a mile (0.4 km) away from Schmucker Hall on Seminary Ridge.[7] Confederate general Robert E. Lee made this stone farmhouse his headquarters for the duration of the Battle of Gettysburg. Thompson cared for wounded men at the house, using her own clothing and bedding to dress their wounds and wrapping the dead in carpets. Visitors who want to learn more about Thompson can take a free tour of the house, which is led by staff from Seminary Ridge Museum. These tours are offered on Fridays in the summer.

CHAPTER SEVEN

THE CIVILIAN EXPERIENCE

Visitors who want to learn more about the Gettysburg area can go to museums that explore the civilian experience of the battle. One is the Gettysburg Beyond the Battle Museum. Here, visitors experience hands-on exhibits that feature artifacts, photos, and documents. The museum helps visitors understand that life in Gettysburg began long before the American Civil War.

In the museum's first gallery, *Natural History*, visitors learn about local rock formations and the Mount Joy meteorite, a space rock discovered near Two Taverns, Pennsylvania. They also learn about dinosaurs that once lived in the region. In one interactive exhibit, guests can compare their hands to a dinosaur footprint.

One artifact at the Gettysburg Beyond the Battle Museum is a sign from a tailor's shop. The sign has bullet holes in it from the Battle of Gettysburg.

Other galleries in the Beyond the Battle Museum explore the many people who visited or settled in Gettysburg before the American Civil War. Visitors learn about these people in several galleries, including one called *Native Americans*. Many of the museum's galleries aim to give visitors a hands-on, immersive experience. *Revolutionary America*, for example, includes a tavern in which visitors can sit and listen to authentic conversations.

In *A Growing Community*, visitors learn about the Underground Railroad. This organization of people aided and hid enslaved people who were fleeing from their enslavers. This was considered an act of disobedience, since it was illegal to help enslaved people avoid being returned to their enslavers.

Gettysburg Heritage Center

At the Gettysburg Heritage Center, visitors learn how civilians in Gettysburg survived during the Battle of Gettysburg. One of the center's most popular exhibits is the Cellar Experience. In this experience, visitors gather in a small theater designed to look like a cellar, with beams overhead and small windows on one side. A recorded narration tells visitors what civilians likely heard while hiding in their cellars during the battle. Sound effects make it seem as if soldiers are marching and running past the windows.

Other galleries focus on the American Civil War and its connection to Gettysburg. *Civil War* tells the stories of

The *Caught in the Crossfire* experience takes place in a dimly lit room. Visitors can see flashes of light coming from the windows and feel the floor shake as gunfire sounds play.

local townspeople who fought to preserve the Union. *The War Comes Home* explores what happened once fighting erupted in Gettysburg and what families in the town did to survive. One gallery is an immersive experience called *Caught in the Crossfire.* It simulates the experience of a family whose home was caught in the middle of the battle.

Visitors enter a gallery set up as a typical 1860s home. They see sunlight slanting through damaged blinds and bullet holes in the walls. Pictures have been knocked off the walls, and a half-eaten meal sits on a table in the center of the room. Visitors can hear the recorded voices of family members taking cover in the cellar. The exhibit's creators used information from letters and diaries to make the recording as authentic as possible. To recreate the sounds of gunfire and cannon fire, museum staff recorded the sounds of Civil War–era guns being shot at a firing range.

Two galleries at the Beyond the Battle Museum educate visitors about what happened immediately after the battle. *The Aftermath* describes the destruction that surrounded citizens after the battle. Exhibits include a battle-damaged wall with lead projectiles embedded in it and the Sherfy Farm Witness Tree. The second gallery focuses on Lincoln's Gettysburg Address. Additional galleries explore Gettysburg's post–Civil War history.

Shriver House

To learn more about the civilian experience in Gettysburg, people can visit several historical homes, including the Shriver House. In the 1990s, Nancie and Del Gudmestad wanted to buy a home in the Gettysburg area and use it to tell the story of people who lived there at the time of the battle. Other museums already told the story of the battle itself, but the Gudmestads wanted their museum to tell a larger story. They bought the Shriver House in 1996. They researched the home's history as they restored it.

The house belonged to Hettie and George Shriver. When the couple started building the home in 1860, there was already talk of a civil war. The Shrivers wanted to build a home with space for their growing family and business. The family lived on the first and second floors. George's business, Shriver's Saloon & Ten-Pin Alley, occupied the lower level. A two-lane ten-pin bowling alley was housed in a structure behind the house.

> "[During] the restoration we began to understand the story of the family who lived in there . . . we decided that if you're going to stand on their floorboards, you ought to hear their story.[1]"
>
> *—Nancie Gudmestad, cofounder of Shriver House Museum, on discovering the home's history*

Today, visitors can tour the house. It is set up much as it would have been when the Shriver family lived there.

The Shriver House is located on Baltimore Street. Today, visitors can take a tour of the house with a guide dressed in Civil War–era clothing.

The cellar level includes a kitchen with laundry supplies, such as a washtub, washboard, and irons. The cellar also includes a saloon with a bar for serving drinks and a central table where patrons could drink, eat, and play dominoes.

On the first floor, visitors see a typical 1800s parlor with tables, a fireplace, and sitting areas. Hettie's kitchen is also on the first floor. It includes open storage shelves. These shelves are not the originals, but the Gudmestads found the outlines of the shelves beneath the room's wallpaper. Much of the home's original furniture was destroyed by the Confederates, but Hettie described it well in her letters and diaries. These writings helped the Gudmestads reconstruct and refurnish the home.

On the second floor, visitors can see typical bedrooms of the era. The master bedroom includes a washbasin and dressing table. The children's room, where the couple's

Restoration

The Shriver House remained empty for 30 years before it was purchased for restoration. Because of this, the restoration project involved not only making repairs but also restoring the home to the way it would have looked in the 1860s. This included removing paint from the home's brick exterior. A wide variety of artifacts were found during the restoration process, including letters and paper dolls. Other discoveries in the house included live ammunition, medical supplies, and bloodstains.

daughters Sadie and Mollie slept, features a bed, a cradle, and a chamber pot.

Visitors reach the house's attic by climbing a set of stairs. When they pass through the door into the unfinished part of the attic, they can see how the Battle of Gettysburg affected the Shriver family. Confederate sharpshooters knocked out bricks in the house to make a hole in the wall so they could safely fire at Union soldiers on Cemetery Ridge. Despite this precaution, two Confederate sharpshooters are known to have been killed in the attic.[2]

Visitors to the Shriver House can see numerous artifacts that the Gudmestads found while restoring the home. These include bullets, spectacles, a glass whiskey flask, and medical supplies such as glass syringes. Depending on which time of year they visit, guests can also see a four-square garden much like the one in which Hettie would have grown fruits, vegetables, and medicinal herbs. In winter, visitors can take a special Christmas candlelight tour of the house.

Jennie Wade House

Another historic home that visitors can tour is the Jennie Wade House. Civilian Jennie Wade was killed in this house

The statue in front of the Jennie Wade House depicts Wade holding a loaf of bread in one hand and a pitcher in the other. Wade's grave can be seen at Evergreen Cemetery.

during the Battle of Gettysburg. A life-size statue of Wade holding a loaf of bread stands on the sidewalk in front of the house. The house belonged to Wade's sister, Georgia McClellan, and Georgia's husband.

Wade and her mother arrived at the house before the battle because Georgia was pregnant. She gave birth before the Confederate Army arrived in the area. At the time, it was common for a woman's female relatives to stay with her to help with her newborn baby. The women also helped provide food for the Union Army. The dough Wade was kneading when she was shot was baked the next day, creating 15 loaves of bread for the soldiers.[3]

Unlike many of her neighbors, Georgia could not leave the area or take shelter in her home's cellar. This is because she had had a difficult pregnancy and delivery. Today, visitors can see her bed set up in the parlor with a baby cradle. Visitors who descend into the cellar can see where soldiers laid out Wade's body before she could be buried.

Throughout the house, people can walk through rooms arranged as they would have been in 1863. One room is a kitchen. Upstairs, visitors see a bedroom with a bed, a chest, and a washstand. Another room contains a shaving stand. The home shows that Gettysburg was much more than a place where a battle took place. It was also a place where ordinary people lived and worked.

Children of Gettysburg 1863

Children of Gettysburg 1863 is a museum with hands-on exhibits created for kids. The museum is located in the historic Rupp House, where John and Caroline Rupp lived with their six children at the time of the Battle of Gettysburg. Visitors learn from the experiences of real children and teens who lived in Gettysburg, including William Bayly, Albertus McCreary, Sadie Bushman, and Tillie Pierce. Galleries include *Growing Up in Gettysburg 1863*, *The Soldiers Are Coming*, *Surviving the Battle*, and *Remembering Gettysburg*.

CHAPTER EIGHT

BEYOND THE CIVIL WAR

While the Battle of Gettysburg is an important part of Gettysburg's past, there are many other things to see and do in the town that are not related to the American Civil War. Several local museums and sites, for example, explore the general history of Gettysburg. One is the World War II American Experience Museum. Many people do not know that Gettysburg has a strong connection to World War II.

During the war, a German prisoner of war (POW) camp was located within Gettysburg National Military Park. The prisoners farmed produce there. Another section of the battlefield was home to Camp Sharpe. Here, World War II soldiers were trained in psychological warfare, or ways to demoralize their enemies.

Every year, the Eisenhower National Historic Site hosts a World War II Weekend. This living history event features costumed guides, educational displays, and World War II–inspired activities.

One part of the World War II American Experience Museum is called *The Home Front*. It explores what people did to support the war effort, including civil defense activities, scrap drives, and victory gardens. The museum also shows visitors what life was like before World War II started. One exhibit is a 1941 Sears and Roebuck kit home, which shows how a typical home of the era might have been furnished and decorated with items ordered from a Sears and Roebuck catalog.

A Personal Collection

The World War II American Experience Museum started out as Frank Buck's personal collection. He had collected almost 80 World War II vehicles, along with uniforms, helmets, and other memorabilia.[1] Buck and his wife, Loni, decided to create the museum to help people learn not only about World War II but also about its connection to the Gettysburg region. What started out as a hobby became an educational mission that the Bucks could share with their neighbors and with visitors.

Another section of the museum is *Arsenal of Democracy*. It explores how the United States transitioned from domestic production to manufacturing items that were needed for war, including uniforms, vehicles, and armaments. The museum's collection includes several World War II vehicles, including a tank and a shop truck. The shop truck allowed mechanics to make repairs on the battlefield. It had hand tools, a generator, and torches for cutting metal. Another eye-catching vehicle is the "Follow Me" Jeep, which was used for leading aircraft through unfamiliar areas.

Other exhibits demonstrate how the war affected family life. Several displays feature children's toys from the time. One exhibit includes a rocking horse, a fighter plane pedal car, and child-size military uniforms.

The museum shows that just as the people of Gettysburg worked to feed and support soldiers in their town, Americans during World War II worked to support soldiers fighting overseas. The museum features an American Red Cross Clubmobile that was staffed by female volunteers. This vehicle looks like a food truck with windows that prop open on the side. The volunteers used the windows to serve coffee and fresh doughnuts to soldiers. Clubmobiles were often stocked with

Nazi and Japanese Imperial Artifacts

One display case at the World War II American Experience Museum contains artifacts from Nazi Germany and Imperial Japan. These items include handguns, swords, knives, clothing, and other elements from military uniforms. Visitors may be uncomfortable seeing artifacts from groups that the US military fought against. But a plaque explains why these pieces are exhibited in the museum. It explains that these items explore topics such as nationalism, anti-Semitism, political oppression, and cultural genocide. The plaque states that visitors must pay attention because these things could happen again.

newspapers, magazines, chewing gum, cigarettes, and candy bars.

Eisenhower National Historic Site

Another place to visit in Gettysburg is the Eisenhower National Historic Site. Dwight D. Eisenhower was a career military officer. Because of his skill for planning and strategy, he received several promotions during World War II. He became a general and oversaw the Allied invasion of France. Because being in the military required moving frequently, Eisenhower and his wife, Mamie,

The white, two-story house at Eisenhower National Historic Site was the first home that Dwight and Mamie Eisenhower owned together. The couple gifted the property to the US government in 1967.

dreamed of owning a home—preferably one where Eisenhower could fulfill his ambition of farming.

After Eisenhower retired from the military in 1948, he and Mamie acquired the farm that is now Eisenhower National Historic Site. In 1950, US president Harry S. Truman asked Eisenhower to be the Supreme Commander of the North Atlantic Treaty Organization (NATO). NATO was established after World War II as an organization of nations working together to ensure each other's safety and security.

Eisenhower placed his farm under the management of his friends Arthur and Ann Nevins. He later served as US president from 1953 to 1961. He and Mamie spent weekends and as much time as possible on the farm starting in the mid-1950s. The home is now an official NPS site.

Visitors to the site can see a variety of things, including the home that the Eisenhowers built. The house is full of interesting details such as the hall wallpaper, which depicts the seals of the United States and every state except Alaska. In the home's sunroom, visitors can see the easel that Eisenhower used while painting. This is also the room where his family entertained Soviet leader Nikita Khrushchev in 1959.

In Eisenhower's bedroom, visitors can see a portrait he painted of his two oldest grandchildren. The portrait hangs above the bed.

While exploring the house, visitors learn about the personal lives of the Eisenhowers and see items that belonged to them. One example is Mamie's lap desk. After having rheumatic fever as a child, Mamie had a heart condition and spent several hours a day in bed. Here, she received visitors and wrote letters using the lap desk. Today, it sits in the middle of the bed. Visitors can also enter the General's Bedroom, where Eisenhower took naps in 1955 while recovering from a heart attack.

Outside the house, visitors can walk past various buildings that make up a working farm. Eisenhower raised Black Angus cattle and sometimes brought heads

Gettysburg Tower

The Secret Service agents assigned to protect President Eisenhower at his farm worried about the Gettysburg battlefield. Part of the problem was the number of people who toured the battlefield. The Secret Service agents had no way of knowing who those people were or whom they might need to watch. They asked the park to close an observation tower whenever Eisenhower was at the farm. The tower was on private property and allowed visitors to view the battlefield from 307 feet (94 m) off the ground.[3] The tower was torn down in 2000 when the NPS acquired the land on which it stood.

of state to the show barn to see his prized animals. The bank barn is the oldest structure on the property. It is built partially into the hillside, which is a typical style for barns in the area. The barn is several stories tall and has space for equipment storage, horse stalls, and a carpenter's workshop.

The US Secret Service office was also part of the bank barn. Today, it looks out of place compared with the rest of the rustic structure. The space had originally been a milk house but was converted for the president's Secret Service detail in 1955. Throughout Eisenhower's presidency, eight to ten agents worked each shift in the barn, monitoring the alarm control panel and radio communications.[2] Closed-circuit TV cameras for viewing the grounds were added in the late 1960s.

Visitors who tour the grounds can see Eisenhower's shooting range and putting green too. The farm also has a helicopter pad, since Eisenhower was the first US president to use this form of transportation. Additional buildings at the site include a guest house and a corn crib, where shucked corn was stored.

The Town of Gettysburg

Today, Gettysburg is a thriving community that offers a variety of activities and experiences. Visitors who enjoy shopping or learning about other cultures can visit the town's Christmas Haus, a holiday-themed store that sells traditional German items such as beer steins, nutcrackers, and wooden Christmas trees. At Gettysburg Polish Pottery, people can buy authentic pottery from the Ceramica Artystyczna factory in Boleslawiec, Poland. Shoppers can find pottery pieces with a variety of patterns, some of which feature cats, horses, flowers, and other unique designs.

People who enjoy spending time outdoors can visit several parks in the area. One state park in the region is Caledonia State Park, which covers 1,125 acres (455 ha).[4] It includes hiking trails, a swimming pool, and fishing spots. Kings Gap Environmental Education Center is another option for fans of the outdoors. It offers an orienteering course that teaches people how to use a compass and map to navigate an area. Maps can be found in the foyer of the education building.

Visitors looking for excitement can try out the 1863 Escape Room, which offers three different Civil War–themed escape rooms.[5] People who are interested in scary stories and hauntings can check out the town's many ghost tours, such as Ghostly Images of Gettysburg. Those who love art can explore art galleries in the town.

Caledonia State Park is located between Gettysburg and Chambersburg, Pennsylvania. It includes ten miles (16 km) of hiking trails.

The Ghosts of Gettysburg

Gettysburg offers many activities for visitors who are intrigued by ghosts and hauntings. They can start by visiting the town's Museum of Haunted Objects, which houses a collection of supposedly haunted and cursed objects. These include a typewriter that is said to type by itself in the middle of the night, a doll that guests have seen blink on its own, and a doll with human teeth. Guides lead visitors through the museum, telling the story of each object and warning guests about what happens to those who say they don't believe the stories.

Visitors who are interested in hands-on experiences can sign up for a wide range of ghost tours. One is the Haunted Orphanage Tour, which begins with a walking tour of the neighborhood along Baltimore Street. Guests pass the oldest house in Gettysburg, the Dobbin House. They also pass the National Cemetery and the location of the National Soldiers' Orphans' Homestead.

After hearing stories about the orphanage and what happened there, visitors are led down the building's original stairs to a cellar in which the orphanage headmistress reportedly locked children whenever they misbehaved.

At the Lincoln Into Art gallery, artist Wendy Allen creates modern portraits of Lincoln.

The Legacy of Gettysburg

The Battle of Gettysburg changed the trajectory of the American Civil War, ending a pattern of Confederate victories and helping the Union work its way toward victory. The war did not end until two years after the battle. But what happened at Gettysburg turned the tide of the conflict in favor of the Union.

Even so, the battle took a heavy toll on the town of Gettysburg. It was a thriving community at the time of the battle. The people who lived there had to deal with thousands of dead and injured soldiers as they struggled to plant new crops and repair their homes. Today, visitors to Gettysburg National Military Park and the surrounding region can walk in the footsteps of these people, reliving an important chapter of US history.

> **“Where we see the serenity with which time has invested this hallowed ground, Lincoln saw the scarred earth and felt the press of personal grief. Yet he lifted his eyes to the future.[6]**
>
> ***—President Dwight D. Eisenhower at the ceremony for the 100th anniversary of the Gettysburg Address*”**

ESSENTIAL FACTS

GETTYSBURG NATIONAL MILITARY PARK BASICS

- During the American Civil War, the Battle of Gettysburg was fought from July 1 to July 3, 1863, in Gettysburg, Pennsylvania. The Union Army won, defeating the Confederate troops. This was a turning point in the war.
- Together, both armies suffered between 46,000 and 51,000 casualties. After the battle, civilians, soldiers, and doctors worked to rebuild and care for the wounded.
- A national cemetery was established at Gettysburg to honor the fallen. During the dedication ceremony on November 19, 1863, President Abraham Lincoln delivered his Gettysburg Address. About 3,500 Union soldiers and 979 unknown men are buried at the site.
- In 1933, the National Park Service took over management of Gettysburg National Military Park. The park spans 5,700 acres (2,307 ha). More than 1.5 million people visit every year.

THINGS TO SEE AND DO

- Explore history exhibits and see the cyclorama painting at the Gettysburg National Military Park Museum & Visitor Center.
- Take the self-guided Auto Tour through the Gettysburg battlefield, stopping at important sites along the way.
- Visit the graves at Gettysburg National Cemetery.
- Take the Cupola Tour at the Seminary Ridge Museum.
- Explore immersive exhibits at the Gettysburg Beyond the Battle Museum.
- Learn about Dwight D. Eisenhower's life and presidency at the Eisenhower National Historic Site.

MAP

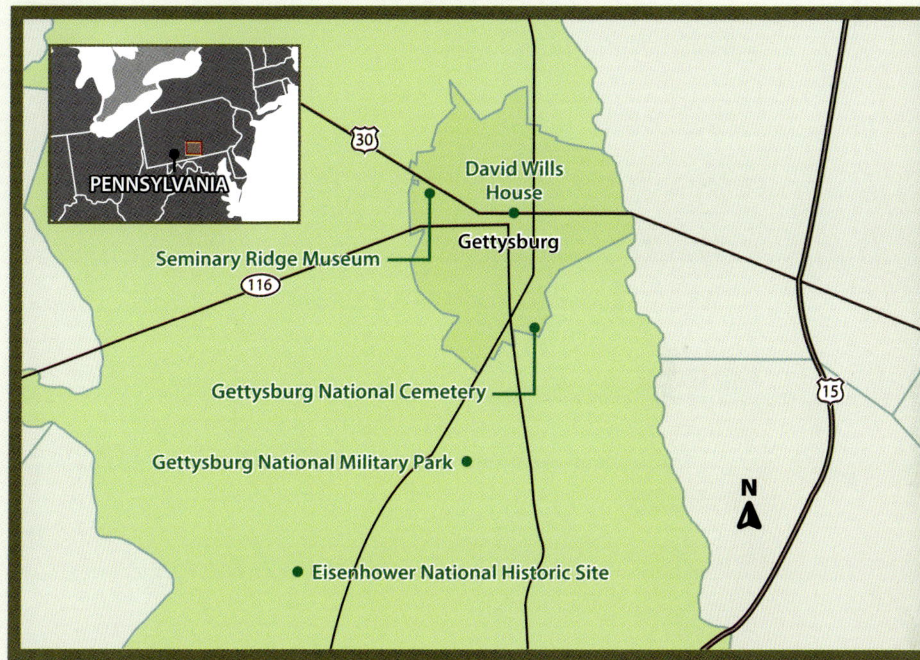

QUOTE

"We see the symbolic story of American peace and plenty living under freedom following a heroic struggle among its own people."

—*Dave Stotts, host of the show* Drive Thru History, *on the Soldiers' National Monument*

GLOSSARY

anesthetize

To give a person anesthesia, or something to make them fall unconscious, in order to perform surgery on them.

armament

A weapon or other equipment used in warfare.

artillery

A large-caliber gun such as a cannon.

carbine

A firearm similar to a rifle but with a shorter barrel.

casualty

A person killed or injured in war.

cavalry

An army unit of soldiers who fight on horseback.

cornerstone

The stone that is laid at a foundation's corner, often the first stone put in place.

cupola

A dome-like structure or turret on top of a larger dome on a building's roof.

demoralize

To cause to lose hope.

enlist

To enroll in the military.

foreground

The area of a scene or painting that is nearest to the observer.

infantry

An army unit of soldiers marching or fighting on foot.

inter

To bury in a grave.

light artillery

Movable artillery pieces such as cannons.

minié ball

A conical lead bullet with a hollow base that was commonly used in the American Civil War.

musket

A long gun used by infantry soldiers that is loaded from the front of the barrel.

secede

To withdraw or leave a union.

seminary

A college that teaches students to be religious ministers.

vestibule

A room just inside the outer door of a church.

ADDITIONAL RESOURCES

SELECTED BIBLIOGRAPHY

"Gettysburg: Virtual Tour." *National Park Service*, 14 Sept. 2022, nps.gov. Accessed 3 Nov. 2024.

Graff, Frank. "Where Did Lincoln Stand during Gettysburg Address?" *PBS North Carolina*, 3 July 2024, pbsnc.org. Accessed 13 Nov. 2024.

Meade, George Gordon. *The Life and Letters of George Gordon Meade, Major-General United States Army*. Vol. 2, Charles Scribner's Sons, 1913.

FURTHER READINGS

Henzel, Cynthia Kennedy. *The War Encyclopedia*. Abdo, 2024.

Nussbaum, Ben, and Gretchen Bacon, editors. *Gettysburg: Three Days That Saved the United States*. Fox Chapel, 2022.

Stanchak, John. *Civil War*. DK, 2023.

ONLINE RESOURCES

To learn more about Gettysburg National Military Park, please visit **abdobooklinks.com** or scan this QR code. These links are routinely monitored and updated to provide the most current information available.

MORE INFORMATION

For more information on this subject, contact or visit the following organizations:

GETTYSBURG BEYOND THE BATTLE MUSEUM

625 Biglerville Rd.
Gettysburg, PA 17325
achs-pa.org/visit

The Gettysburg Beyond the Battle Museum explores the lives of Gettysburg civilians before, during, and after the American Civil War. It features a variety of artifacts and interactive exhibits.

GETTYSBURG NATIONAL MILITARY PARK MUSEUM & VISITOR CENTER

1195 Baltimore Pike
Gettysburg, PA 17325
gettysburgfoundation.org/exhibits-tours-events/museum-visitor-center

The Gettysburg National Military Park Museum & Visitor Center is the first stop for most visitors at the park. It is home to the Gettysburg Museum of the American Civil War, a cyclorama painting, and other exhibits. Guests can also get park maps at the Visitor Center.

NATIONAL CIVIL WAR MUSEUM

1 Lincoln Cir.
Harrisburg, PA 17103
nationalcivilwarmuseum.org

The National Civil War Museum strives to tell as complete a story of the American Civil War as possible. Its exhibits explore causes of the war, the roles of women during the war, how armies were created, and other topics.

SOURCE NOTES

CHAPTER 1. THE BATTLE OF GETTYSBURG

1. "Map of US in 1860." *Museum of the Cape Fear Historical Complex*, n.d., museumofthecapefear.ncdcr.gov. Accessed 22 Jan. 2025.
2. "Map of US in 1860."
3. "War Declared: States Secede from the Union!" *National Park Service*, 19 Sept. 2023, nps.gov. Accessed 22 Jan. 2025.
4. "Chancellorsville." *American Battlefield Trust*, n.d., battlefields.org. Accessed 22 Jan. 2025.
5. "Gettysburg." *American Battlefield Trust*, n.d., battlefields.org. Accessed 22 Jan. 2025.
6. "Abraham Bryan a Testament to Resilience." *Tillie Pierce House Inn*, 29 Mar. 2024, tilliepierce.com. Accessed 22 Jan. 2025.
7. Ian Webster. "Value of $1,028 from 1863 to 2024." *CPI Inflation Calculator*, n.d., in2013dollars.com. Accessed 22 Jan. 2025.
8. Ian Webster. "Value of $15 from 1863 to 2024." *CPI Inflation Calculator*, n.d., in2013dollars.com. Accessed 22 Jan. 2025.
9. "Abraham Bryan a Testament to Resilience."
10. "Gettysburg."
11. "The Second Day at Gettysburg." *NPS History*, 29 June 2024, npshistory.com. Accessed 22 Jan. 2025.
12. "Pickett's Charge." *American Battlefield Trust*, n.d., battlefields.org. Accessed 22 Jan. 2025.
13. "Gettysburg."
14. "Battle History." *Gettysburg Pennsylvania*, n.d., gettysburgpa.gov. Accessed 22 Jan. 2025.
15. "Pickett's Charge."
16. "The Jennie Wade House: History." *Gettysburg Battlefield Bus Tours*, n.d., gettysburgbattlefieldtours.com. Accessed 22 Jan. 2025.
17. "The Battle of Gettysburg: How Area Residents Dealt with the Carnage." *Mercury*, 24 Sept. 2021, pottsmerc.com. Accessed 22 Jan. 2025.
18. "How Area Residents Dealt with the Carnage."
19. "How Area Residents Dealt with the Carnage."
20. "How Area Residents Dealt with the Carnage."
21. "The Soldiers' National Cemetery at Gettysburg." *American Battlefield Trust*, n.d., battlefields.org. Accessed 22 Jan. 2025.
22. "The Soldiers' National Cemetery at Gettysburg."
23. John Mitchell Vanderslice. *Gettysburg, a History of the Gettysburg Battle-Field Memorial Association*. The Memorial Association, 1897. 204–205.
24. "Commemorating Gettysburg National Military Park." *Conservation Fund*, n.d., conservationfund.org. Accessed 22 Jan. 2025.
25. "Edward Everett." *National Park Service*, 18 June 2015, nps.gov. Accessed 22 Jan. 2025.

CHAPTER 2. THE VISITOR CENTER AND MUSEUM

1. "Gettysburg: Visitor Center." *National Park Service*, 21 Mar. 2024, nps.gov. Accessed 22 Jan. 2025.

2. "Visitor Center."
3. "Creating the Cyclorama." *Battle of Gettysburg Cyclorama*, n.d. battleofgettysburgcyclorama.com. Accessed 23 Jan. 2025.
4. "Gettysburg: Cyclorama Painting." *National Park Service*, 15 Sept. 2022, nps.gov. Accessed 22 Jan. 2025.
5. "Cyclorama Painting."
6. "Gettysburg: Collections." *National Park Service*, 27 July 2023, nps.gov. Accessed 23 Jan. 2025.
7. "Ranger Programs at Gettysburg." *National Park Service*, 4 Dec. 2024, nps.gov. Accessed 22 Jan. 2025.
8. "Ranger Programs."
9. "Sachs Covered Bridge." *VisitPA*, n.d., visitpa.com. Accessed 22 Jan. 2025.
10. "Daily Ranger Programs at Gettysburg." *National Park Service*, 5 Nov. 2024, nps.gov. Accessed 22 Jan. 2025.

CHAPTER 3. THE BATTLEFIELD

1. "Gettysburg: Places." *National Park Service*, 17 Oct. 2024, nps.gov. Accessed 22 Jan. 2025.
2. "Gettysburg: Virtual Tour." *National Park Service*, 14 Sept. 2022, nps.gov. Accessed 22 Jan. 2025.
3. "Gettysburg: Frequently Asked Questions." *National Park Service*, 22 Apr. 2024, nps.gov. Accessed 22 Jan. 2025.
4. "Monuments and Markers." *National Park Planner*, 21 Jan. 2025, npplan.com. Accessed 22 Jan. 2025.
5. "Monuments and Markers."
6. Marnie Hunter. "Two Houses on Gettysburg Battlefield Available for Overnight Stays." *CNN*, 13 May 2024, cnn.com. Accessed 22 Jan. 2025.
7. "Virtual Tour."
8. "Eternal Light Peace Memorial." *National Park Planner*, 19 Jan. 2025, npplan.com. Accessed 22 Jan. 2025.
9. "Virginia State Memorial." *National Park Planner*, 8 Sept. 2022, npplan.com. Accessed 22 Jan. 2025.
10. "Little Round Top." *National Park Planner*, 20 Jan. 2025, npplan.com. Accessed 22 Jan. 2025.
11. "91st Pennsylvania Infantry Monument." *National Park Service*, 29 Apr. 2022, nps.gov. Accessed 22 Jan. 2025.
12. "Tour Stop #9—The Wheatfield." *National Park Service*, n.d., nps.gov. Accessed 22 Jan. 2025.
13. "Antietam: The Signal Corps." *National Park Service*, 15 Sept. 2023, nps.gov. Accessed 22 Jan. 2025.
14. "Plum Run." *National Park Planner*, 9 Sept. 2022, npplan.com. Accessed 22 Jan. 2025.
15. George Gordon Meade. *The Life and Letters of George Gordon Meade*. Vol. 2, Charles Scribner's Sons, 1913. 129.

SOURCE NOTES CONTINUED

16. "The Pennsylvania State Memorial." *Gettysburg Battlefield Bus Tours*, 20 Sept. 2011, gettysburgbattlefieldtours.com. Accessed 22 Jan. 2025.

17. "Tour Stop #13—Spangler's Spring." *National Park Service*, n.d., nps.gov. Accessed 22 Jan. 2025.

18. "Meade's Headquarters (The Leister Farm)." *Civil War Stuff*, 14 Apr. 2023, civilwarstuff.com. Accessed 22 Jan. 2025.

CHAPTER 4. NATIONAL CEMETERY

1. Rob Wingert. "'Simple Grandeur': The Creation of the Soldiers' National Cemetery." *NPS History*, n.d., npshistory.com. Accessed 22 Jan. 2025.

2. Wingert, "'Simple Grandeur.'"

3. Wingert, "'Simple Grandeur.'"

4. "John F. Reynolds." *Stone Sentinels*, n.d., gettysburg.stonesentinels.com. Accessed 22 Jan. 2025.

5. "National Cemetery Virtual Tour." *National Park Service*, 1 May 2023, nps.gov. Accessed 22 Jan. 2025.

6. "Lincoln Address Memorial." *National Park Service*, 23 Sept. 2022, nps.gov. Accessed 22 Jan. 2025.

7. "Gettysburg Address." *National Park Service*, 22 Jan. 2025, nps.gov. Accessed 22 Jan. 2025.

8. "Gettysburg Memorial Cemetery." *YouTube*, uploaded by Drive Thru History with Dave Stotts, 13 May 2022, youtube.com.

9. "Soldiers' National Monument." *Historical Marker Database*, 3 June 2020, hmdb.org. Accessed 22 Jan. 2025.

10. Wingert, "'Simple Grandeur.'"

11. "Soldiers' National Cemetery." *National Park Planner*, 29 Oct. 2022, npplan.com. Accessed 22 Jan. 2025.

CHAPTER 5. HISTORICAL SITES IN GETTYSBURG

1. "Washington to Gettysburg Battlefield." *Rome2Rio*, n.d., rome2rio.com. Accessed 22 Jan. 2025.

2. Karlton Smith. "A Presidential Trip to Gettysburg." *NPS History*, n.d., npshistory.com. Accessed 22 Jan. 2025.

3. "Ticket to the Past—Unforgettable Journeys." *Gettysburg Foundation*, n.d., gettysburgfoundation.org. Accessed 23 Jan. 2025.

4. Smith, "A Presidential Trip to Gettysburg."

5. "David Wills House 3D Tour." *National Park Service*, 6 Jan. 2021, nps.gov. Accessed 23 Jan. 2025.

6. "David Wills House." *National Park Service*, 24 Oct. 2024, nps.gov. Accessed 23 Jan. 2025.

7. "Take a Walk in President Lincoln's Gettysburg Footsteps." *Destination Gettysburg*, n.d., destinationgettysburg.com. Accessed 23 Jan. 2025.

8. "Another Baltimore Street Witness Tree." *Gettysburg Daily*, 14 Jan. 2009, gettysburgdaily.com. Accessed 23 Jan. 2025.

9. "Home." *Gettysburg Witness Trees*, n.d., gettysburgwitnesstrees.com. Accessed 23 Jan. 2025.

CHAPTER 6. SEMINARY RIDGE MUSEUM

1. Chris W. Lewis. "Gettysburg from the Top." *HistoryNet*, 11 Oct. 2019, historynet.com. Accessed 23 Jan. 2025.
2. Lewis, "Gettysburg from the Top."
3. "Cupola Tour and Museum Admission." *Seminary Ridge Museum and Education Center*, n.d., seminaryridgeeducation.org. Accessed 23 Jan. 2025.
4. Stanley B. Burns, MD. "Civil War Medical Practice." *PBS*, n.d., pbs.org. Accessed 23 Jan. 2025.
5. "Preserving the Accounts of Men and Women Who Made History: Seminary Ridge." *YouTube*, uploaded by Americana Corner, 28 June 2023, youtube.com.
6. "Slavery in the Land of the Free." *ThingLink*, 2023, thinglink.com. Accessed 23 Jan. 2025.
7. "Experiences." *Seminary Ridge Museum and Education Center*, n.d., seminaryridgeeducation.org. Accessed 23 Jan. 2025.

CHAPTER 7. THE CIVILIAN EXPERIENCE

1. "Gettysburg's Bloodstained Sniper's Nest." *YouTube*, uploaded by The History Underground, 20 June 2021, youtube.com.
2. "What to See." *Shriver House*, n.d., shriverhouse.org. Accessed 23 Jan. 2025.
3. "The Jennie Wade House: History." *Gettysburg Battlefield Bus Tours*, n.d., gettysburgbattlefieldtours.com. Accessed 22 Jan. 2025.

CHAPTER 8. BEYOND THE CIVIL WAR

1. Paul Wiseman. "New Museum Opens in Gettysburg." *HistoryNet*, 31 Aug. 2021, historynet.com. Accessed 23 Jan. 2025.
2. "Secret Service Office: Eisenhower National Historic Site." *Historical Marker Database*, 7 Feb. 2023, hmdb.org. Accessed 23 Jan. 2025.
3. Deb Kiner. "Gettysburg Tower Demolished in 2000." *PennLive*, 3 July 2017, pennlive.com. Accessed 23 Jan. 2025.
4. "Caledonia State Park." *Destination Gettysburg*, n.d., destinationgettysburg.com. Accessed 23 Jan. 2025.
5. "1862 Escape Room." *Destination Gettysburg*, n.d., destinationgettysburg.com. Accessed 23 Jan. 2025.
6. Chris Mackowski. "Ike, JFK, and the Gettysburg Address." *Emerging Civil War*, 28 Mar. 2017, emergingcivilwar.com. Accessed 23 Jan. 2025.

INDEX

ABOUT THE AUTHOR

SUE BRADFORD EDWARDS

Sue Bradford Edwards is a nonfiction author who has written more than 30 Abdo titles, including *Trench Warfare*, *The Bombing of Pearl Harbor*, and *American Life in the 1970s*. She is passionate about history and often visits Fort Davidson, an American Civil War site in Missouri, with her family. They've also recently visited Fort Davis, Texas, home of the Buffalo Soldiers. Edwards writes about history, social justice, and science from her home office in Saint Louis, Missouri.